ONE WEEK LOAN

**black dog
publishing**
london uk

Black Dog Publishing
London UK © 2008

The author and photographers
have asserted their moral
right in the work comprising
How to be a Happy Architect

All rights reserved
Written by Irena Bauman
Printed in the European Union

Black Dog Publishing
10A Acton Street
London WC1X 9NG

T: +44 (0)207 713 5097
F: +44 (0)207 713 8682
E: info@blackdogonline.com
W: www.blackdogonline.com

British Library Cataloguing-in-
Publication Data

A catalogue record for this
book is available from the
British Library

ISBN: 978 1 904772 78 1

Black Dog Publishing is an
environmentally responsible
company. *How to be a Happy
Architect* is printed on G-Print
and Munken Lynx, both
Elemental Chlorine Free and
FSC certified papers.

BaumanLyons
Architects

You say what you think needs to be said.
If it needs to be said, there are going to be
a lot of people who will disagree with it,
or it would not need to be said.
Herb Lock

**Bauman Lyons Architects
Leeds, December 2007.**

D0514234

We all have the right to say
NO
to making bad places.

When I am working on a problem I never think about beauty. I only think about how to solve the problem. But when I have finished, if the solution is not beautiful, I know it is wrong.

Buckminster Fuller

How to be a Happy Architect

In this book we have tried to capture the thoughts borne out of our collective experience of practising architecture in the context of contemporary British culture.

We hope it will resonate with other practitioners, shed some light on the dilemmas we encounter in every aspect of architectural practice, and offer hope for those who are struggling to resolve them. The understanding that may arise from this is also intended to inspire students and some, if not all, professionals.

All of us are faced with personal dilemmas about who to love, how to be nicer to one's parents, when and whether to have children, how to reduce one's eco-footprint but still travel to nice places, which channels to watch, which newspapers to read, when to restart our exercise routine since the last one lapsed six months ago, and how not to miss all those fabulous cultural events that always seem to finish just as we find out about them.

We do so in the context of global dilemmas over which we feel we have increasingly less control, such as growing social inequality, the demise of political and civic engagement, climate change, and an increased fear of everything from contaminated eggs to terrorist attacks.

In addition to all that, architecture is practised against a backdrop of continuous rapid change and the consequent multiple systems of disconnections it creates. These manifest themselves as a sequence of dilemmas that haunt contemporary architectural practice. The following list is neither exhaustive nor in any specific order of importance, but it represents the complexity of daily decisions we have to make:

- Global or local or both?
- Artist or businessman or both?
- Quick fix or long-term solution?
- Individual stardom or member of a team?
- Theory and/or practice?
- Commercial imperatives or social needs or both?
- Image and/or content?
- Pencil and/or CAD?
- Creative integrity or democratic consensus or both?

These choices pull us in different and often incompatible, directions and in doing so create disconnections of thought and process. Such disconnections are made more difficult to repair by the sheer speed of change, which is not within our power to even fully comprehend, let alone control.

Those speed-induced disconnections are further exacerbated by:

- The conflicting agendas of clients, users and architects themselves
- The oppositional needs of quality, time and money
- The distorted values imposed by the media
- The shift from citizenship to consumerism
- Constant social and technological change
- Political short-term expediency versus long-term needs
- The proliferation of delivery mechanisms
- Increasing layers of middlemen
- Hypocrisy and gaps between rhetoric and actions.

Architects have the capacity to think on a variety of scales and handle complex data. We are problem solvers with a regard for aesthetics, and as such we have a vital contribution to make, to the job of stitching together these multiple disconnections.

The following chapters explore private choices over which we have an influence; the state of our profession, over which we should exercise more influence; and the fundamental issue of for whom we choose to work, which is where our influence should be exercised to its utmost but seldom is.

Happiness is an elusive emotion and yet it drives all our actions. As a dynamic team that constantly changes without losing its general direction, we have concluded that the only route to professional happiness for us is through the identification of our role as stitcher of disconnections and a reasonably uncompromised adherence to it. If our stitching attempts fail we still have the option to say NO to the creation of further disconnections. Furthermore, these skills are urgently needed to help us adapt to the biggest and most rapid change yet, that of climate. As a profession we are poorly placed to utilise our skills to their full potential. We are out of touch with public opinion, disengaged from each other within the profession, inadequately educated, and too pre-occupied with self-promotion and celebrity status. Can we change this?

Recent decisions we have made in an attempt to connect disparate strands of our practice to the needs of a sustainable society:

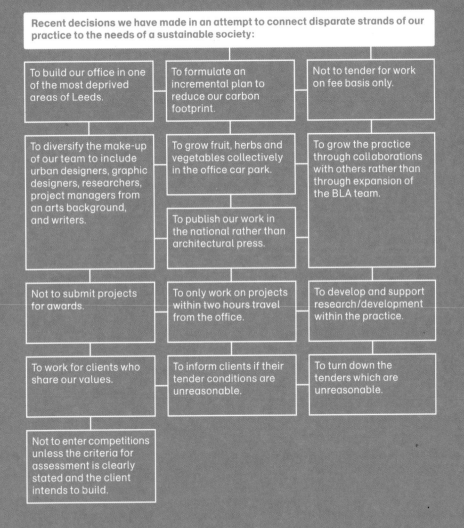

To build our office in one of the most deprived areas of Leeds.

To formulate an incremental plan to reduce our carbon footprint.

Not to tender for work on fee basis only.

To diversify the make-up of our team to include urban designers, graphic designers, researchers, project managers from an arts background, and writers.

To grow fruit, herbs and vegetables collectively in the office car park.

To grow the practice through collaborations with others rather than through expansion of the BLA team.

To publish our work in the national rather than architectural press.

Not to submit projects for awards.

To only work on projects within two hours travel from the office.

To develop and support research/development within the practice.

To work for clients who share our values.

To inform clients if their tender conditions are unreasonable.

To turn down the tenders which are unreasonable.

Not to enter competitions unless the criteria for assessment is clearly stated and the client intends to build.

Who makes our cities?

Leeds City Centre, UK: All British cities are developed through a sequence of disconnected initiatives that the current planning system is too weak to stitch together into a coherent story.

Who designed this?

Who paid for this?

... or this?

Who consented to this?

... or this?

Who consented to that?!

Provocation:

Any architectural project we do takes at least four or five years, so increasingly there is a discrepancy between the acceleration of culture and the continuing slowness of architecture. The areas of consensus shift unbelievably fast; the bubbles of certainty are constantly exploding.

Rem Koolhaas

The degree of Slowness is directly proportioned to the intensity of memory; the degree of speed is directly proportioned to the intensity of forgetting.

Milan Kundera, *Slowness*

Architecture today is a pluralist practice, one that oscillates between fantasy and realism.

Jean-Louis Cohen

Introduction:
Architect as the Stitcher of Disconnections

In this book we suggest that architects, having developed their skills of analysis, strategy, design and the ability to visualise, have the capacity to perceive, understand and stitch together the multiple disconnections caused by the exceptionally rapid rate of change.

In the first chapter we will consider three areas of disconnections: those within architectural practice, those within client bodies and those within cities themselves.

We have identified just a fraction of what we experience on a daily basis. However, there is already a universal awareness of the constant inefficiencies and obvious inconsistencies arising from these disconnections, so our focus is not on whether disconnections exist, but on their nature, quality, characteristics and what we are able to do about them.

Provocation:
Many People believe that architecture is a 'Homo Universalis' a 'Renaissance man' while in fact, he continuously is confronted with his painful lack of knowledge. Travelling as a tourist through different programmes of his clients, he acquires just enough information to simulate expertise and avoid exposing his superficiality. He is not popular because he is constantly trespassing on the territory of other professions.

To seek an outlet for his urge to debate, he is condemned to teach. He teaches in order to gather knowledge rather than mediate it. From teaching, he develops the skill and alertness to 'surf' through an ever accumulating mass of knowledge and ideas, which no individual could master in a lifetime, not even within a single profession.
Kees Christiaanse

Change is impacting on every aspect of architectural practice. As we were packing to move to our new purpose-built studio after ten years of leasing, we had the ideal opportunity, whilst purging all items of huge sentimental value, to reflect on the extraordinary changes that have taken place in every aspect of office, city and personal lives within what is by all standards a short period in history:

We can no longer park outside the office as professionals have moved into the neighbourhood; the whole area has shot up in price and is full of new bars and cafes; and young, affluent 30 somethings—mainly women—have displaced an elderly population, because the area has become desirable.

Post does not arrive in the morning. When it finally gets here in the afternoon it contains mainly Amazon DVD rentals, Civic Trust letters and a lot of unsolicited mail. Other deliveries—big computer boxes, car-share cars, ebay orders and collections of recycled and sorted waste—signify new shifts in work style.

We rarely need to sign letters. Filing has disintegrated since there are multiple archiving methods. All communications are increasingly informal, nobody spells correctly and we have just got rid of the single emergency office tie as dress code is also becoming increasingly informal.

A significant proportion of staff work less than a five day week to allow for other interests, including teaching and family. Childcare is shared by both sexes and the younger staff members are pushing having children well into their mid and late 30s. Many of the younger staff live in shared professional households and more of them are making a decision to live with their parents into their adult life to allow them to recover from university debts. All of this reflects nationwide trends.

We increasingly employ other consultants. SAGE has transformed accounting and we have daily bank statement updates. The bank manager exists but only as a monthly payment of ten pounds. He/she has changed so frequently that we have given up on contact. We have one drawing hot-board and our computers in the last ten years have metamorphosed from floor boxes with 21 inch screens to laptops with double flat screens. We have a computer replacement programme of 18 months rotation and we have long accepted it as the ongoing overhead as opposed to a one-off capital investment. There is on average a ten per cent loss of efficiency because of computer gremlins and we all find ourselves bereft of purpose when the server goes down.

Communications within the studio are mainly by email and we are constantly having to regulate the use of social networking and instant messaging as the silver bullet has not yet appeared that allows us to incorporate these new ways of communication into our everyday work routine and productivity. The tapedeck was replaced by minidiscs, then by CDs and then by a computer-based music library with so much choice (all legal) that we do not have it on very much. Headphones are the norm.

The increase in job extranets requires memorising ever-increasing numbers of passwords and user names, and an ever-increasing pressure to absorb vast quantities of information. Response time is now instant, while the volume of information received at any one time has increased exponentially. The limitations of the Outlook culture are, it seems, only the capacity and speed of the human brain.

The laptop has become an extension of the body, allowing for international hot-desking, 24 hour working, on tap presence and response (so appreciated by all clients), simultaneous private and professional communication and all entertainment not involving movement. The boundary between work, home and playtime is truly blurred.

Small and discrete clubs have formed in the zone between work and home, composed of those who can be trusted to respond to emails at all hours of the day and every day of the week. After-hour response takes on the significance of the Masonic handshake. And our IT manager is the most important member of staff, with the power to create nothing less than a gorge of disconnection. By that token he is the greatest stitcher of us all. Information and knowledge are everywhere and on tap—which is just as well since we need to know more about everything all the time. Our staff make-up has diversified and now includes researchers, graphic designers and illustrators— and we are only 20 or so strong. Some of us have acquired additional skills such as health and safety, first aid and project management. The office is international and multi-lingual.

We threw away our technical library three years ago. Magazines still arrive but are rarely read beyond headlines. Instead they are viewed almost entirely online. Samples are never kept and the CD-based technical information service has been replaced by a web library. This is another reason why we sit idle when the server goes down.

Most of the project tasks are implemented either through the computer or through collaborative meetings. The average time spent at one's desk is 30 per cent of a working week, except for the young architects. The rest of the time we are on the road or in the meeting room.

Choice of staff is dictated by their knowledge of specific computer programs. Students are expected to be totally proficient in them.

Project teams have become bigger as skills, due to their complexity and rapid rate of change, become vested in an ever-increasing range of specialists. It is usual to have a project manager, planning supervisor, energy consultant, BREEAM consultants, artist agency, artist, artist's solicitor, marketing consultant, business planner, fundraiser, community consultants, conservationist, commercial agents, housing agents, ecologist, access consultant, planning consultants, development consultant, fire strategy consultant and retail consultant all involved in the development of a project. Previously there would have been only an architect, quantity surveyor and an engineer.

As we have tried to make sense of the shifting context, process and content of architectural practice we have found one quality of the profession of architecture which has stayed constant: our creativity.

Architects' creativity is their strongest asset. Knowledge can now be acquired by the smallest of offices, but creativity is a gift that cannot be accessed on the web. This is our stitching tool.

Architects are greatly disadvantaged if they do not have a good grasp of all the areas of expertise now required to deliver the built environment. In that context, Kees Christiaanse's pessimistic statement is a challenge rather than a condemnation. However, architects are totally stripped of added value if they merely 'follow the orders' without injecting creativity into the process. In this respect Kees Christiaanse misses the point of architectural contribution altogether.

And now all this creativity is most urgently required to deal with the biggest and most all-encompassing driver of change, which is altering the nature of architectural design. Climate change poses a profound, urgent and global challenge and it is the architectural profession that needs to change to respond to it. However, with many individual and wonderful exceptions 'the profession' in general appears to be less than inspired by this challenge to its creativity.

Architects are very well placed to spearhead the required shift of the built environment culture, but we need to understand it first ourselves. Too little attention has been paid in architectural schools to the issues relating to climate change and many practising architects are failing to question environmentally discredited building forms.

We are still churning out deep plan buildings, offices with air conditioning, north-facing apartments and acres of car parking.

Architectural profession has to change and adapt once again, and the pressure on architects is to lead by example if we are to influence clients.

In the following chapters we examine the factors that conspire to slow down the change within the architectural profession just when it is most needed.

Architect's office pre-1995

Architect's office post-1995

In my experience, if you have to keep the
lavatory door shut by extending your left
leg, it's modern architecture.
Nancy Banks-Smith

Architects are pretty much high-class whores.
We can turn down projects the way they can
turn down some clients, but we've both got
to say yes to someone if we want to stay
in business.
Philip Johnson

The physician can bury his mistakes, but the
architect can only advise his client to plant
vines — so they should go as far as possible
from home to build their first building.
Frank Lloyd Wright

Not many architects have the luxury to reject
significant things.
Rem Koolhaas

The next set of disconnections relates to clients. Clients come in a variety of shapes and forms. Many projects that don't turn out as well as they could have, have a history of faulty decision-making running throughout the delivery process. Architects could play a vital role in improving projects from the outset by applying their knowledge and experience to ensure that the essential ingredients of a sustainable, good quality scheme are incorporated into the client brief.

Before we jump in to work on a competition entry, tender or any other proposition, we should set the project up to succeed by ensuring that the fundamental proposition is sound in all respects.

This may require a set of initial questions to the client. Some of these are applicable to all clients; others will vary with the client sector. If a satisfactory response to all initial questions were a condition of acceptance of a commission, a whole host of disconnections further down the line would be minimised.

In our practice we have identified the common as well as sector-specific causes of disconnections and have learned to cross-examine projects from the outset in an attempt to mend the torn connections and patch up the missing thinking. When this appears to be impossible we do not take on the project.

Our clients can be broadly grouped as private developers, public bodies, communities of end users and private clients. All of these groups use one of three methods of selecting an architect for each project: tender, design competition or direct appointment. Each client type and each method requires pre-commission examination of potential disconnections. Each client and method has some inherent inbuilt connection that makes him or her desirable for different reasons.

Private Developers

Desirable connections:
In general private sector developers have clearly stated goals to make a profit from property development. They are pro-active risk takers, energetic, motivated and major contributors to growth of the economy. They tend to work in small teams, form long-term collaborative relationships with the design team that enhance clear lines of authority and communication and reduce the need for bureaucracy to the bare minimum. They tend to be pragmatic and focused on delivery. Some developers have made use of good designers to produce a differentiated product on the market.

Most common sources of disconnections:
Most of the disconnections in working with private developers are created by their desire to maximise profits in a short period of time. The projects are often speculative, making it impossible to respond to user requirements. They are often built in an available rather than desirable location, frequently without suitable infrastructure in place.

The desire to maximise the profits drives developers to overdevelop sites whilst reducing the development time, thus leaving inadequate design and thinking time. Budgets are often too low to secure good quality or are inappropriately spent on expensive materials that are used as 'makeover' tools in an attempt to disguise standard commercial buildings.

In recent years, on the back of a long period of strong economy, a trend has emerged of major developers employing high-profile architects to design commercial buildings—thereby enhancing commercial value and obtaining planning permission for what might otherwise have been considered an overdevelopment of the site. This trend has been especially notable in the procurement of tall buildings. Ambitious men and women searching out equally ambitious men and women to deliver their flagship work is the most common union behind such projects. This fashion-sensitive trend has put some of the most able architects in the Western world in the service of profit maximisation and made them complicit in creating an unsustainable approach to city growth.

Commercial and residential agents, key advisors to developers, are guided by what has been selling. Although well placed to identify and maybe even create new markets, they often choose, conservatively, to lead developers to provide a single type of accommodation—and are thus jointly responsible for a lack of variety and differentiated products on the market.

1.2

Civic benefits negotiated by local authorities as a 'tax' on commercial developments, diverted towards the public realm, affordable housing and other such social benefits, effectively relieve developers from their responsibility to act civically. We no longer have the benefits of businessmen wishing to contribute to the town or city through the quality of their development that may last for many centuries and help to reinforce the identity of the place.

The most effective strategy for architects to deal with such potential disconnections is to establish some influence over as many matters as possible pertaining to the projects. This includes knowing the site context, knowing the local political scene, understanding competition from other projects in the pipeline, understanding local, regional and national policy as well as forthcoming policy changes. It also means being well connected to local networks, well informed globally and increasingly, being able to understand what constitutes a sustainable future.

Early establishment of authority allows architects to interrogate the brief, the budget, the composition of the design team and the programme. It also helps to secure mutual trust between the client and design team in the early stages of the project, thus reducing opportunities for further disconnections.

This process is difficult to achieve when architects and / or their clients work at a great distance from each other and from the site. The geographic distance leads to disconnections of knowledge and of emotional investment, exposing the projects to the possibility of poor decisions.

Our cities are increasingly built through these kinds of processes, and the most profound contribution to mending such disconnections that architects can make is to commit to working locally.

Public and Private Quango Clients

Desirable connections:
In a democracy, public bodies are elected to serve public needs.They are motivated by the desire for a just society and ordered communities. They are well-networked, accountable and at least in theory, take a long view on their investments. Most common causes of disconnection are demonstrated in the illustration opposite.

Due to their accountability, public sector clients are, in general, risk-averse. Many of their processes, especially the selection of design teams, are subject to equal opportunities legislation–a single factor that has made the greatest contribution to disconnections in the urban environment procurement.

The 'rotation' list of approved consultants used by most local authorities when tendering small jobs, the framework agreements used to support the capacity of local authorities whilst reducing the need for constant tendering and the Official Journal of European Union (OJEU) procurement process used for bigger projects, are hopelessly flawed and almost guaranteed to result in an inappropriate team. None of these selection methods takes account of design quality, teamwork, established networks and supply chains, local empowerment and incubation of local capacity and above all, the knowledge of the place where the project is to be built.

This method disconnects the right teams from the right jobs and fails to tap into the energy of local supply chains who have enormous design talents and energy, but cannot meet the irrelevant criteria that is asked for because these are so onerous. To deal with complexity of disconnections in the public client sector requires constant pro-active feedback from the architects to their clients as well as the resolve by the design team to refuse to participate in projects that are fundamentally flawed from the outset. Feedback is difficult to convey since the leadership is not clear and as seen above, clients are sometimes difficult to define.

The most effective remedy available for an individual is to make their feedback known, make constructive suggestions and refuse to support such processes by joining in the bidding.

It is not possible for an architect or even a single architectural firm to significantly influence and improve the current flaws in public sector projects procurement. Such an improvement can only be achieved by collective action. Until bodies such as the RIBA find the improvement of clients' commissioning procedures a suitable cause for campaign, there is little chance of mending the present disconnection.

Public Sector Clients
Knowing who the client is
in the public sector can be
complicated as they are
often multi-headed.

Most common causes of disconnections:
Knowing who the client is in the public sector can be complicated
as they are often multi-headed. A department that owns the client's
site is often different to the one who has written the brief and
commissioned the project. And other departments again lay claim
to different aspects of the project. Asset management requires
capital receipts from the site, the procurement unit requires the
architect to consider health and safety policy, equal opportunities
policy, environmental policy and most recently disaster policy.
Housing and neighbourhood require a public consultation. In addition
there are the political agendas, rarely fully understood by the design
teams, exacerbated by the lack of continuity as the chief executives
hop from one new initiative to another and the staff take extensive
sick and flexi-leave to cope with the stress of crisis management
arising from under-funding and frequent policy changes. Added to
this is the need to work to politically-driven funding timescales that
rarely correspond to the timescales required for capital projects.

Assessment of risks associated with public sector clients—some questions to ask before getting involved:

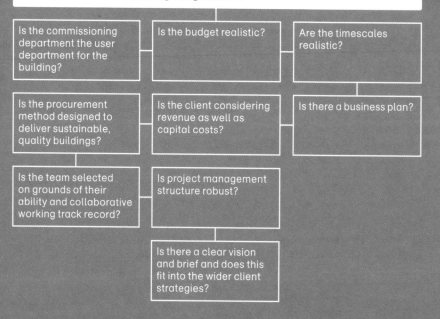

Is the commissioning department the user department for the building?

Is the budget realistic?

Are the timescales realistic?

Is the procurement method designed to deliver sustainable, quality buildings?

Is the client considering revenue as well as capital costs?

Is there a business plan?

Is the team selected on grounds of their ability and collaborative working track record?

Is project management structure robust?

Is there a clear vision and brief and does this fit into the wider client strategies?

If any of the answers are negative, work with the client to re-align them—or don't get involved.

Communities of Users as Client

Desirable connections:
User groups and communities make rewarding clients as the architects are offered the opportunity to respond directly to the user brief and offer their skills to fulfil the client's needs and ambitions.

The client groups are often motivated, visionary and committed. They understand their own needs and are in a strong position to question ideas when these are in conflict with those needs. They are rooted in their locality and believe that the project will contribute to making their place better. In most successful cases there is a true collaboration with the design team who are seen as the essential tool for delivering the client's vision.

Most common causes of disconnections:
Working directly with user groups can be hugely rewarding but also humbling. Often architects are ill-equipped to provide the range of services that may be required. Our education, with notable exceptions, is short on student exposure to such projects.

Our presentation and communications skills are developed for delivery of vision and justification of design decisions as opposed to a debate and conversation. Community groups can frequently find this type of communication patronising and laden with value judgments alien to their own perspective.

The architect's position as the 'outsider' to the user group further fuels the possible mistrust, which can be one of the greatest disconnections within the project procurement. We are unlikely to ever match the local knowledge of the place or the use for which we are designing, we are therefore at a high risk of getting it wrong.

Community clients are not always well organised, nor do they necessarily speak with one voice. Local politics and personal squabbles can get in the way of sound decision making, clear instructions and trust. Furthermore, for most groups a capital project is a once in a lifetime experience and architects often find themselves in roles as facilitators and educators—for which education, once again, has not given adequate preparation.

Disconnections also arise between the aspirations of the community and what can actually be achieved with the inadequate funds usually available. There is also a disconnection between the expectation of the benefits the investment will bring and the reality, since physical environment alone cannot make a substantial difference to marginalised communities.

The middle class ideal of empowering the powerless is well meant, but requires a multi-faceted approach to deprivation and a long-term commitment. That is, policy must be made for the long-term and the near total lack of this over the past few decades has created the biggest disconnection of all. Architects alone cannot close this gap.

It is essential for architects to have the right skills before they embark on such a project. Delivering the construction of buildings is only one of very many skills that are required to deliver successfully within this sector. Our strategies in mending the skill gaps are to both supplement and to learn new skills. Supplementing the architectural team includes the appointment of many new skilled people to the design team, including business planners, fundraisers, consultants, community workers, researchers, graphic designers and artists. Such people can help us bridge the major disconnections between the respective cultural worlds of the client and the design team and the disconnections between architects' education and the required skills for the job.

It is also essential to invest in learning new skills within the team. These include learning new ways of communicating ideas, such as through film and storytelling; learning about funding systems; researching the political make-up of the place where the project is located; negotiation and conflict resolution skills; facilitation techniques; and research techniques which include gaining an understanding of demographic, social and economic data.

Getting Clients through Design Competitions

Desirable connections:
It is a widely held belief within the architectural profession that competitions are good for creating high quality projects and even better for promoting young talent.

Many well organised competitions are indeed just that. They offer the advantage of commitment by the client to good design from the outset. They also offer other opportunities: to learn through a creative challenge; to work with visionary clients and the opportunity for publicity.

They often require design integrity and intellectual effort that more mundane projects are not able to offer. It could be argued that they offer an opportunity for architects to match their interests closely to those of the client by choosing to compete in some but not other competitions.

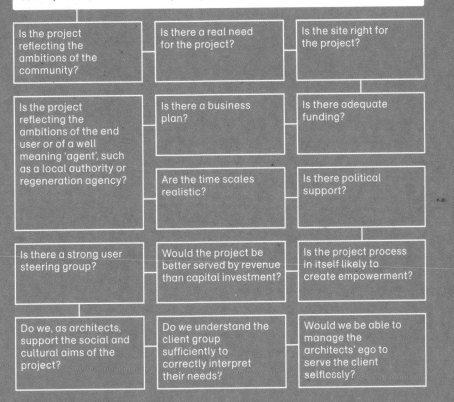

**Assessment of risks associated with community clients—
some questions to ask before getting involved:**

Is the project reflecting the ambitions of the community?

Is there a real need for the project?

Is the site right for the project?

Is the project reflecting the ambitions of the end user or of a well meaning 'agent', such as a local authority or regeneration agency?

Is there a business plan?

Is there adequate funding?

Are the time scales realistic?

Is there political support?

Is there a strong user steering group?

Would the project be better served by revenue than capital investment?

Is the project process in itself likely to create empowerment?

Do we, as architects, support the social and cultural aims of the project?

Do we understand the client group sufficiently to correctly interpret their needs?

Would we be able to manage the architects' ego to serve the client selflessly?

Most common causes of disconnections:

Competitions exist because architects allow them to. We are taught to compete and to excel throughout our entire education. Competitions provide the opportunity for this competition culture to continue into adult life forever.

Architects persistently offer their most precious asset, their creativity, free of charge in the hope of winning competitions. The odds of winning are very low. But our inquisitiveness, our creativity and our vanity continue to create a disconnection between the high value of what is produced and the low chance of an award. Our vanity in particular makes it acceptable for us to produce large amounts of excellent work in return for the possibility, no matter how remote, of instant distinction, visibility and maybe even fame.

Competitions are often badly run and have been known to end in big blunders. Problems have been known to include bad briefs, unclear assessment criteria for onerous requirements, lack of follow-through after the competition and dismissal of the winning team.

It could also be argued that procuring a design solution, often at a great distance between the designers and the site and the consequent lack of local knowledge, is the leading reason why national or international competitions are not the best procurement methods of good schemes. Perhaps the only exceptions are iconic buildings that are notoriously freed from the concerns of local relevance because they themselves become that relevance.

However, the harvesting of keen talent and the resulting publicity is appealing to many clients for whom the competition can be a source of cheap publicity and a way of finding an exciting design solution. Furthermore, the elements that are vital and common to all successful schemes, namely the compatibility of the client with the design team and the compatibility of the design team members with each other, are the very ones that are not delivered through the design competition route.

Many architects recognise the clients' lack of accountability as well as the exploitative nature of architectural competitions and periodically call for the profession to boycott them. Such calls, even from the most authoritative figures, meet with deadly silence from the profession that has lost its ability to share a collective view.

Competitions will not disappear as long as we crave them.
Architects can, however, be selective and choose the competitions
that offer opportunities to investigate important issues that are
compatible with their area of interest and knowledge and are
likely to result in the designs actually being implemented.

We can also respond to some of the calls for boycotting the most
exploitative practices. At the most fundamental level we can insist
on being paid for participating and being rewarded adequately for
winning entries. In our ideal, happy world, all competitions would
be of a limited kind and would be used by the clients to find the
best team rather then the best design.

Choosing the client who can make you happy.
As architects we can be too eager to please to consider whether a
given opportunity is the one we want or need. We agree to tender
when conditions are unfair, we accept flawed briefs and we often
do not care if the business plan for the project makes any sense.

The possibility that architects could make a beneficial impact
on the quality of the built environment by taking proactive action
to refuse to work on poorly conceived projects, remains untested
since we don't often say NO nor do we ever take collective action.
Except at award ceremonies where our vanity is celebrated and
our worst work is conveniently overlooked.

"Competitions exist because architects allow them to. We are taught to compete and to excel throughout the entire education system. Competitions allow the opportunity to continue into the adult life forever."

Competition re-run is next chapter of library saga
Ellen Bennett

Richard Rogers Partnership has already designed a scheme for the library—at a cost of £280,000—but it was ditched after internal political wrangling at the council.

Earlier this year, Glenn Howells Architects, Adjaye Associates and Make were appointed to come up with concepts for the scheme, at a cost of £12,000, but it now appears that these too have been abandoned (News,17 March). The council is still looking for an "iconic" scheme with a "strong identity".

Building Design
8 September 2006

Simpson's contest boycott call ignored
Will Hurst

In the email Simpson argued that participation would "undermine our value as architects" because it did not offer payment for the work involved. The RIBA competitions office advises clients to pay an honorarium to architects in invited design competitions.

"It is regrettable that practices are prepared to countenance working with people who clearly have little respect for that they can offer" said Simpson. "None of us mind working hard but if you are not going to get any costs and you might have need for five architects working on (the competition)… then I just think it is doing a disservice to the profession."

Building Design
26 August 2005

Causeway for concern
Richard Waite

A major blunder by the organiser of one of the most popular competitions in recent years is threatening to turn the contest into a farce.

It is understood that the hapless official unintentionally 'copied in' all the contestants into an email, allowing the entrants to see who they were up against.

The Architects' Journal
21 July 2005

1.2

The Trouble with Competitions

Rem demands boycott
Ellen Bennett

Rem Koolhaas has called on architecture's superstars to join him in a campaign to overhaul the competition system, which he has condemned as "hideous" and a drain on resources and influence.

"We are letting ourselves be drained of endless resources and huge amounts of ideas – all to no avail", said Koolhaas. "I am on a campaign now to convince the world that this kind of competition is hopeless and that we should find more efficient forms of architectural competitions against each other."

"It is amazing how the best brains in the profession can be manoeuvred into a position of complete weakness when they should be in a position of strength."

Building Design
5 January 2007
bdonline.co.uk

The competitions gamble
Zoë Blackler

For a young or unknown, the odds of winning one of these gems are not great, and the risks of taking part are high. But if you know the rules of the game, you too could triumph in the competitions gamble.

Building Design
21 October 2005
bdonline.co.uk

Official Journal of the European Union

OJEU tender conditions can reach absurd dimensions of disconnection between the nature of required information and the needs of the project.

We often question the tender requirements but rarely get a response from the client body—this letter was sent twice but was never acknowledged or answered despite us chasing an answer on two occasions.

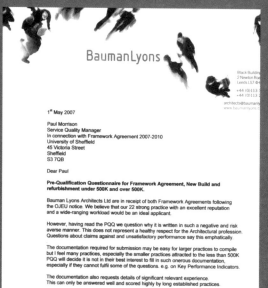

Bauman Lyons Architects Ltd are in receipt of both Framework Agreements following the OJEU notice. We believe that our 22 strong practice with an excellent reputation and a wide-ranging workload would be an ideal applicant.

However, having read the PQQ we question why it is written in such a negative and risk averse manner. This does not represent a healthy respect for the Architectural profession. Questions about claims against and unsatisfactory performance say this emphatically.

The documentation required for submission may be easy for larger practices to compile but I feel many practices, especially the smaller practices attracted to the less than 500K PQQ will decide it is not in their best interest to fill in such onerous documentation, especially if they cannot fulfil some of the questions. e.g. on Key Performance Indicators.

The most innovative, creative, value for money, environmentally sustainable Architecture is being carried out by Architects who would like to be asked about the quality of their buildings rather than ' have you got a disaster strategy' in place. For me this type of PQQ is a disaster strategy in itself.

Letter from Simon Warren Director, BLA 1 May 2007

Why is it so hard for young architects?
Patrick Lynch

Public bodies and even arts clients demand "Show us your turnover. What's your track record?" before any mention is made of design. It seems as if nobody can be bothered to be a patron of architecture. And the same old cabal of RIBA committee members blithely pass on work and awards to each other, as if we didn't notice or were too scared to say anything.

Building Design
13 October 2006

The great fat cat stitch up
Ellen Bennett

More than three quarters of all major public building projects advertised in the Official Journal of the European Union in the last year were won by practices that were more than 20 years old and had more than 20 staff.

Of the 133 architectural contracts advertised in the journal between July 2004 and July 2005. Just 6% were won by practices that had been established for 10 years or less, and just 11% by practices of 10 people of fewer.

Building Design
11 November 2005

History of Woodroyd Centre Project Managers

	2002	2003	20
Project Manager 1			
Project Manager 2			
Project Manager 3			
Project Manager 4			
Project Manager 5			
Project Manager 6			
Project Manager 7			
Project Manager 8			
Project Manager 9			
Project Manager 10			
Project Manager 11			

1.2

The Discontinuity of Transient Project Managers

Project managers are often subcontracted by the clients to large management firms—there is no culture of long-term commitment to the project and the PM often jumps jobs. This can happen several times over the life of a project leaving the architect to provide the continuity and brief sequential project managers so that they can then manage the architects.

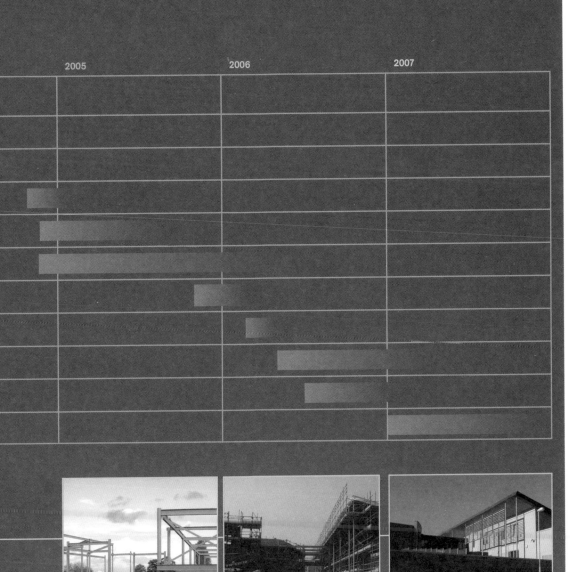

2005   2006   2007

The lesson which architects should learn from the long chronicle of lofty dreams and abominable disasters which combine to form the history of modern architecture, is that the prime secret of a 'good city' is the chance it offers people to take responsibility for their acts 'in a historically unpredictable society' rather than in a dream world of harmony and predetermined order.

Zygmunt Bauman

This doesn't imply that architecture should aim at reproducing banal spaces that function in silence. As modern art, photography and cinema have shown, many avenues lead to poetry. One simply goes through the almost effortless revelation of the déjà-là, of what is 'already there'. But collision, collage, and contrast are also poetic instruments, and I cannot imagine the future city as shaped by only calm, 'realistic' buildings or only by dynamic, deconstructive labyrinths, or even less by sleek glass boxes.

Jean-Louis Cohen

Every city has probably two or three hundred committees. Every committee is dealing with just one problem and has nothing to do with the other problems.

Alvar Aalto

The rate of change and the consequent disconnections in policy and delivery manifest themselves in the physical environment. It is common for cities to change and adapt, for buildings to accept new functions and for new cultural activities to overlay historic ones. It is inevitable that sequential industries and employment patterns will make their mark on the urban fabric. We are familiar with textile mills becoming apartments, building society headquarters converted into bars, trams replaced by buses and buses replaced by trams again.

Much has been written about the rapid expansion of cities as well as the phenomenon of shrinking cities. Some cities adapt better than others. The ability to absorb change appears to be a combination of the flexibility of inherited urban infrastructure and the priority given to historic continuity and the understanding of its relation to the identity of the place.

During the last 50 years few cities have managed to protect themselves from the impact of disconnection arising from the increased speed of change, which is wiping out our collective memory of what we know already about good place-making.

On the following pages are various examples of diverse types of disconnection collected on my travels. It is possible to find all of these examples and more, in every contemporary city with the possible exception of those historic cities whose communities have never forgotten their identity nor the relationship between nature, and that which is man-made.

Every city has probably two or three hundred committees. Every committee is dealing with just one problem and has nothing to do with the other problems.

Alvar Aalto

Disconnections caused by economic forces:
disconnections of poverty

Council Housing in Armley, Leeds, overlooking the booming city centre—an illustration of the profound disconnections in the fabric of the city caused by 'no go areas' where poverty is associated with danger.

1.3

**Disconnections caused by
changing governance and policy shifts:
change of policy**

The last school in the city
centre of Leeds was closed
and converted into offices
in 1999, the year in which
the government published
its Urban White Paper
calling for regeneration and
densification of city centres
through provision of
residential accommodation.
The boom that followed
failed to attract families into
the city centre due to lack
of family provisions such
as schools.

Administration boundary
of two different authorities
with different bicycle lane
provision, Freiberg, Germany.

Disconnections caused by
changing governance and policy shifts:
change of governance

Leeds Civic Hall: the
processional entrance is
mostly closed. Millennium
Square was reinvented in
2000 as an entertainment
venue. The relation between
the building and its context
is now disconnected.

1.3

**Disconnections caused by
changing governance and policy shifts:
mono policies**

The history of government housing
policy can be read in one small area
of Holbeck in Leeds. Terrace of the
1890s, high rise of the 1960s, Rayburn
estates from the 70s and the housing
associations of the 80s, each one
developed as if the previous one was
not there already. Disconnected
identity follows the physical
disconnections.

Disconnections between vision
and implementation:
disconnections caused by
organisational structures

The Barnsley Master Plan
by Alsop Architects. Visions
are often used to raise the
profile of regenerating areas
but this marketing exercise
can set expectations which
are difficult to match in the
pragmatic world of delivery.

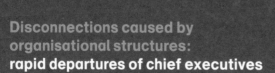

Disconnections caused by
organisational structures:
rapid departures of chief executives

An unfinished flyover at
University of East London.
The change of the chief
executive stopped the
development of this
flyover, commissioned
by his predecessor. It
remains unfinished to
this day hovering above
the new campus.

Disconnections caused by
organisational structures:
rigid organisational structures

Bus Stops can't be moved
(Metro)

Can't fix to the soffit
(Network Rail)

Access for inspection
required at all times
(Network Rail)

Can't fix to the walls
(Network Rail)

Width of lanes fixed
(Highways Department)

Utilities can't
be moved

Constraints imposed by
two different monopolies.
Network Rail and the
Highways Agency make
some of our worst spaces
difficult to improve.
These organisations are
oblivious to the impact
of their indifference.

1.3

Disconnections caused by
organisational structures:
departmental silos

51

Three kilometres of highway
pedestrian bridges in Leeds—
a poor apology for major
disconnections between
communities and the city
centre through relentless
programme of highway
construction since the 1960s.

1.3

Disconnections caused by organisational structures: **disconnections between capital and revenue funding**

The Museum of Popular Music, a Millennium project delivered in haste after a major competition, was closed within nine months of opening. The business plan never worked. As with the Millennium Dome, there were insufficient visitors and inadequate revenue streams programmed.

1.3

Disconnections of
civic ambition:
iconic statements in a
profit-driven culture

The development of a
flagship civic concert hall
in Gateshead, England,
is eventually surrounded
by mediocre housing
developments provided
by the highest bidder
and accepted by the city
keen to see investment
at any cost. This is a
reminder that the private
sector needs the public
sector to drive the agenda
of good design.

1.3

**Disconnection through
lack of judgement:
inappropriate planning control**

These buildings were
constructed in Leeds in
the 1980s, at a time when
the planning department
supported a concept of
postmodern vernacular
nicknamed "The Leeds
Look". It created a total
disconnection between
function and architectural
expression.

1.3

Disconnection through
lack of judgement:
misuse of public art

Some examples of very
bad public art dotted
around Leeds and
procured, presumably,
as an apology for the
very bad buildings.

1.3

Disconnection through lack of judgement:
cultural misunderstandings

Leeds Millennium Square blasting out the summer Olympics to a non-existent audience on a hot Sunday afternoon in 2004. Siena the next day on an overcast Monday afternoon with nothing going on. While designing the public realm in England we ignore the fact that we have different cultural habits of behaving in public.

1.3

Disconnection through
lack of judgement:
disconnection of fear

CAR
PARKING
FOR
RESIDENTS
ONLY

WHEEL
CLAMPING IN
OPERATION

The deprived communities
which are often physically
disconnected from the
rest of the city are also
separated by fear.

Constructing Excellence report calls for new wave of megapractices and says RIBA is out of touch

Profession takes a beating

Charlie Gates

The architecture profession is out of touch, marginalised, leaderless and economically fragmented, according to a damning report from one of the construction industry's leading reformers.

The report, which calls for the creation of "mega-practices", has been compiled from 200 hours of consultation with more than 50 industry leaders including senior figures from design watchdog Cabe, airports body BAA, the Department for Trade & Industry and large practices including BDP, KPF and Edward Cullinan Architects.

It highlights the criticisms levelled at architects by the construction industry and will be used by the RIBA as a "route map" for reforming the profession to win back lost influence.

The report, by Constructing Excellence chairman Bob White, claims the profession "is noted for its introverted perspective where architects are driven by their own achievements and peer group recognition rather than responding to client and market needs". It claims architects still see themselves as "struggling artists" and says the RIBA is seen as "out of touch."

It also controversially calls for practices to consolidate to form more efficient and reliable "mega-firms" to deliver large public projects. This echoes a call made in 2002 by former RIBA president Paul Hyett for practices to merge. Deals to gear up for major public projects include the recent purchase of the Percy Thomas Partnership by Capita, Aukett's takeover of Fitzroy Robinson and SMC Group's purchase of a string of medium-sized practices.

Former BDP head Richard Saxon backed the call for mega-firms and urged practices to get bigger or continue to miss out on major projects.

"The best way for architects to get opportunities is to become associates or partners in larger firms," he said. "It is laughable when you look at the lack of opportunities architects in their 30s have when they are not part of large practices. The idea that big equals boring is not true. It is fuelled by the cult of schools and their design heroes. If we do not do this work someone else will."

But Adam Caruso of small design-led practice Caruso St. John said mega-firms would compromise design quality.

"The US has had a mega practice tradition over the last 20 years and every major public building in recent years has gone to a European architect," he said.

The report has also sparked a debate over the future of archi-

Knocked for six

● Profession has fragmented economic structure.
● Architects plagued by "struggling artist" introspection.
● Education is weak and needs a total overhaul.
● Architects are marginalised from PFI.
● The profession lacks leadership.
● The RIBA is "out of touch".

tectural education. It calls for a "total overhaul of the system rather than incremental change" to deliver more business and technically savvy students. It also urges practices to become more involved in education.

The idea was rejected by Christopher Cross, secretary of school heads group Schosa. "The industry wants oven-ready chickens that can instantly fit industry demands, but many people think education provides more than just that. Education has other considerations," he said.

RIBA president Jack Pringle also rejected the report's recommendations on education. "The comments are a bit off beam," he said. "There is no doubt education will change, but the schools are not getting it wrong, they just need more support from practices."

The architecture profession is out of touch, marginalised, leaderless and economically fragmented, according to a damning report from one of the construction industry's leading reformers.

The report by Construction Excellence chairman Bob White, claims the profession "is noted for its introverted perspective where architects are driven by their own achievements and peer group recognition rather than responding to client and market needs". It claims architects still see themselves as "struggling artists" and says the RIBA is seen as "out of touch".

Profession takes a beating
Charlie Gates

Building Design
30 September 2005

Introduction:
Whose Value System?

As a graduate student entering architectural practice I felt an outsider and that feeling lasted for many years. Looking back, I spent these years relearning, rethinking and acquiring the skills that were not offered at my school of architecture but were essential for happy practice.

This process of rethinking included having to dump the educational baggage that included journalist-led architectural role models and the learned response to defend, rather than debate, designs. I came to learn instead that architects work, not compete, in teams with other architects and with other people—including clients—who have a different approach, complementary knowledge and a diversity of agendas.

I got to know a new set of disciplines hardly mentioned throughout my architectural training: quantity surveyors and project managers, for example, challenged design decisions because they were inefficient, expensive and unpractical, as opposed to unexciting, lacking in theoretical basis and not beautifully drawn.

I had to learn that users of buildings valued 'adequacy for purpose' as well as—or possibly more than—aesthetic qualities. I learned that the language architects used and the drawings we showed, often alienated the client group and that the aspirations of the architect were secondary, in the main, to that of the client: excellent architecture is possible only if the client wants it and bad architecture is implemented because the client consented.

My early encounters with the professional institution did not immediately offer gateways into happiness either. When gathered together, professionals displayed then, as now, a larger-than-average amount of the most undesirable by-product of architectural education: vanity. What I found on closer inspection was an insider group preoccupied with the politics of the architectural profession and an outsider group preoccupied with fees and getting jobs. The two groups found common ground in name-dropping and in critical appraisal of absent fellow members. I guess these traits are common to all creative sectors, and the ego plays a vital role in the creative processes. The issue for happy practice has been, therefore, not how to eliminate the ego but how to tame it.

Contemporary postgraduate architectural education is based on 1980s author-centred practices rather then on certain subjects or problems. Student seem to go to postgraduate schools looking to become the next great prophet of architecture. But they don't realise that the statistical probabilities of that happening are very small, and further, that even the greatest figures need to develop a considerable capacity to understand the situation in which they operate and its relationships with their field of interest.

In this sense, I don't think that the 1980s 'à la carte' postgraduate education is able to generate solid knowledge for use outside of the institutions, and worse, produce over-educated professionals who are unable to engage productively in anything for several years, doomed beneath the weight of their own personal visions.

Alejandro Zaera-Polo

2.0

Individually, architects are exceptionally able professionals. But just as siblings cannot overcome their childhood relation to each other in their grown-up years, so our education causes us to revert to the learned default competitive behaviour every time we gather together or present ourselves within a team. The pressure to 'get it right' which is the backbone of architectural education conditions us to be certain even when all evidence around us points to the plurality and complexity and choice of certainties.

It is these perceptions that lead to our examination of how our education system and the streak of vanity are, between them, holding back the profession from responding to the changing needs of our society.

The slow response of both architectural educationalists and the architectural profession to changing needs is causing an additional set of disconnections. It requires each individual architect to forge their own meaningful path based on their own value system, since an alternative collective path either in education or within the profession is not available.

The danger of isolation that such an approach once implied is no longer an issue since we now have the ability to connect to other like-minded individuals all over the world and from all sorts of forums at the push of a button. It is this access to a huge variety of thought that already allows students to bypass their teachers and professionals to bypass their institutes, as both the teachers and institutes become detached from the issues that architects most want to tackle.

So it may be that the disconnections between education and practice can continue to be corrected and re-aligned in the process of practising and that the disconnection between the professional body and its membership be bypassed altogether. But these current disconnections are the cause of a great deal of waste and loss of creative energy as it is less effective to act individually than to act collectively.

It is the lack of collective architectural stance, beyond the glamour of awards, that is the most glaring omission from current debates. The following three chapters examine the source of this absence as we consider the disconnection caused by the slow response to required changes in education, professional bodies and opinion-formers on architecture, and suggest some possible changes that may help to stitch these back together.

Vanity or genius?
Uncompromising architectural
hero Howard Roark portrayed
by Gary Cooper in the film
The Fountainhead.

Chapter 2.1
The Curse of Howard Roark:
Disconnections between Education and Practice

It is a constant puzzle how the role model of an uncompromising, heroic, self-absorbed designer, epitomised by Howard Roark in *The Fountainhead*, still has appeal in the British architecture scene. The appeal is, however, subliminal rather than overt and most practitioners are in denial of its existence. 15 years of political correctness have seen to that. Roark's was the kind of architecture upon which the profession—represented by historians, journalists, teachers and architects—bestows the highest accolades. It is a kind of architecture which reveals a deep attachment to the old-fashioned model of single authorship of 'uncompromised' work.

The beginning of this doctrine's reign is easy to trace, as the 18 year olds who have been reared on a diet of glamourous iconic architecture selectively portrayed by the lifestyle media, enter the architectural education system. There they meet teachers who will shape them for years to come.

Whereas there is little debate in England (compared to other European countries such as Holland, Denmark, Austria and Germany) on what and how architecture should be taught, there is no debate at all on who is doing the teaching. In other university subjects, the selection of teachers is based on their academic track record and the depth of their knowledge. The quality of their published work provides evidence of the knowledge they have accumulated and can pass on to their students.

It is difficult to trace the criteria by which tutors of design, the prime focus of architectural education, are selected and appointed, since a large proportion of design teaching is done by people who have never practised, or who have left practice. Nor have many of them followed an academic career—the traditional route into teaching in other university subjects. The only credentials to teach appear to be that they themselves were taught in a school of architecture. This is equivalent to saying that an A-level student can teach an A-level class.

There is no doubt that some tutors have a gift for inspired teaching, an ability that is rare and intuitive and cannot be obtained through any quantity of formal training. But such teachers, although they definitely exist in schools of architecture, are few and far between.

... Well I could say that I must aspire to build for my clients the most comfortable, the most logical, the most beautiful house that can be built. I could say that I must try to sell him the best I have and also teach him to know the best. I could say it, but I won't. Because I do not intend to build in order to serve or help anyone. I don't intend to build in order to have clients. I intend to have clients in order to build.

The Fountainhead by Ayn Rand
Howard Roark in conversation with the Dean of the Institute of Architecture following his expulsion from the school for ignoring the accepted canons of architectural style.

You probably don't want to hear this, but it is time we stopped talking about architecture. We need to get out of the gilded box we build ourselves into.

We should think about educating, training and celebrating developers.

The challenges of the future are so much more complex and system-based that the object culture architecture currently embraces... So long as architects self-marginalise by purposefully excluding the business of development and its real burden of complexity and decision making from their business, architecture will remain a gentleman's weekend culture.

Bruce Mau—Manifesto, Icon issue 050 August 2007

The majority of design tutors are self-taught and make it up as they go along. Design teacher training is generally not thought necessary—and is not generally available.

Some of the disconnections between education and practice that cause such a shock to students on entering the profession—many of whom leave within five years—are caused by the value system they inherit from teachers unfamiliar with the reality of practice. Lacking practical experience or formal architectural education training, those tutors do the only thing they can: they pass on what they have been taught, even if this is no longer what the architects of the future need to know.

Students describe University tutors, England 2008:

Male, mid-late 40s, English:
Architect. Very practical approach to architecture, as you would expect from a practising architect. Quite elusive as he was a busy man, big disadvantage for people on his project.

Male, mid-late 30s, New Zealand:
Set up a practice virtually straight out of university with mates. Became embroiled in litigation for a few years over defective works on one of the projects, left the practice to become a tutor. Moved to teach in England. Became disillusioned with politics of university and British weather. Everyone thought he was a bit weird at first but grew to love him. Close relationship with pupils, came on social events with us. Appreciated his honesty and kindness (a good combination for a tutor). Inspirational, very conceptual. Doesn't care much for engineers.

Male (Dr), mid-late 40s, English:
Nice man but hopelessly tactless. I have never known someone to be so cruel, to so many different people, without meaning to! Very old fashioned approach to architecture. Very well educated in a proper sense— appreciated Fine Art, the writing of Ruskin and classical architecture. Loathed computers and brushed stainless steel, preferring stone and craft. I suspect he secretly believes that there is no place for women in architecture, or in a university for that matter.

Female, mid-late 40s, Finnish:
Part time tutor who worked more than full time hours. Very difficult to understand a lot of the time due to suspect English skills. Advocated a very typical Scandinavian approach to architecture – obsessed with timber. Prominent figure in the studios, enjoyed being around the students in the thick of it.

Harvard takes perfectly good plums as students, and turns them into prunes.
Frank Lloyd Wright

If we don't want students to take frozen snapshots of today's ideas out into the world, we need to cultivate a culture of intellectual scepticism that encourages imagination, enquiry and experimentation. The key to survival today is continual learning—revising, reworking, and upgrading constantly.
Stan Allen

Students seem to go to post-graduate schools looking to become the next great prophet of architecture. But they don't realise that the statistical probabilities of that happening are very small, and further, that even the greatest figures need to develop a considerable capacity to understand the situation in which they operate and its relationships with their field of interest.
Alejandro Zaera-Polo

Visiting critics

There is a tradition in most schools of visiting practitioners contributing to design review sessions. Many who do so provide a welcome connection between education and practice and make a significant contribution to learning by offering their practical knowledge and experience.However, the teaching practitioner may on occasions regress into his/her own student mode, in search of the creative freedom they lost since they started practising, and teach as they were taught rather than as they have learned in practice. They have the privilege of influencing students without the responsibility for their continuous development.

The practitioner is also sometimes motivated to teach by a desire to learn from the students and talk about their own work to sustain their profile among the younger generation and less by their commitment to the students themselves.

As there does not appear to be a formal process of selecting visiting tutors, their invitations are often based on the personal contacts of the teaching staff who use their subjective judgement to make this selection and do not need to account for it.

Part-time teachers

The percentage of full-time tutors has been gradually falling, despite student numbers tripling in the last few years. Meanwhile the number of part-time tutors is rapidly rising.

There are many practising architects who wish to close the gap between theory and practice. The benefits of having such teachers are tremendous but the pitfalls are just as great. It is not possible to run a practice on a part-time basis so the 'teaching practice' usually consists of small, often experimental projects outside of the mainstream commercial pressures which may be very exciting and design orientated but are nevertheless not representative of the full range of architectural experience.

Alternatively, part-time practitioners are young, uncompromising designers waiting for their big break and teaching in the meantime to support themselves. They can make great enthusiastic and creative teachers but they have no experience of practice to pass on. Once again, these teachers only have theoretical knowledge to offer.

One more variant is the part-time practitioner whose practice is run by other directors or partners, thus disengaging the teaching partner from all the responsibilities of running a practice and building buildings.

And then, of course, there are the ex-architects who do not want to work full-time and so enter academia because part-time work is not a realistic option for practice. These teachers find jobs in education off the back of their practice profile at the point where they can no longer feed it and grow it. Their teaching from then on is based on a frozen point in time—a dangerous condition in a fast-changing context.

Visiting and part-time teachers can find their position unsatisfactory as they miss the decision-making and rarely meet with the full-time staff to discuss the direction of teaching and the adjustments that may be needed. Part-time practitioners should, in theory, be able to close the gap between education and practice, but in reality their ability to do so is limited.

Full-time tutors.
Full-time design tutors are often practitioners who did not get on with the process of practice. No research has been done on who teaches architecture, so our assumptions are just that. They are based purely on limited observation and can and should, therefore be challenged and debated. But it seems practitioners leave practice for teaching either because they found it limiting or because they found it difficult. They are attracted to a world where creativity is less constrained and architecture can still be a dream. And this is how they teach it.

Once in the system, teaching staff do not seem to need to undergo any teacher training, nor are they obliged to undertake compulsory CPD as the practitioners do. And there are new challenges for design tutors as academia in general moves rapidly towards a funding award system based on assessment of the department's research record.

Architecture, positioned in a no man's land between science and art, does not seem to be always understood by university deans. Furthermore, as architectural tutors are taking on the challenge of fitting architectural teaching into an academic straightjacket, less time is available for the actual teaching. This does not appear to alarm the universities as teaching quality has been sidelined as irrelevant to status, accreditation and funding requirements within higher education.

These conditions are unfavourable for design teachers, who need to be flexible, agile, open-minded, inquisitive, all-embracing generalists and most importantly available to teach students.

2.1

What is actually taught also requires debate. The nature of teachers and the lack of teacher training impacts on architectural education, as whole new areas of knowledge, which arguably should be led by universities, are actually altogether missing. Currently there is precious little evidence of schools being concerned with futurology or drivers of change such as global warming–surely one of the most significant changes to impact on architectural practice over the next decades. And yet, in most schools environmental sustainability is still covered only in a token series of lectures, when it should be integrated into the very fabric of architectural thought.

Other notable omissions in design teaching seem to be the very areas most commonly found in practice: refurbishment and housing work, for example, barely feature in most schools.

There is no doubt that architectural training needs to provide students with a foundation layer of essential knowledge, including appreciation of design. But at the moment most architectural training is weighted in favour of design excellence, disproportionally to the needs of society. This is captured in a very narrow definition and applied largely to preferred building types such as arts centres and other civic buildings, but excludes the majority of the built environment, which consists of housing and commercial buildings.

And the disconnection between education and practice grows even greater when considering that there are many different roles architects can and do, take on, and not all of them require exceptional design skills.

Architects are often exceptional strategists, good team leaders, and inspiring and visionary in their understanding of how places work. They are good technicians and solve problems creatively through lateral thinking. They are often socially motivated and committed to what they do. They constantly work with large budgets and collaborate with large and complex teams.

The skills they need are broader than design ability and yet many of the techniques required in diverse practice, such as research skills, leadership skills, management techniques, business planning sense, conflict resolution skills, understanding of funding streams and understanding of politics and policy, to name but a few, are not taught at all.

How can architecture be taught today?

In the context of the laboratory, the first task I would conceive of is the observation of the processes at work in today's cities, including the analysis of the social, technical, and the aesthetic performances of architecture. We need a more reflexive, self-critical, but also more generous architecture, architecture without compromise in terms of its intrinsic qualities; but also without compromise in its duty to serve, and to protect against injustice and domination.

How should one practise architecture?

The most innovative, the most critical design cannot be confused with scientific research—the production of knowledge. In this respect, research is now a widespread component of architectural culture, and a vital part of education.

Jean-Louis Cohen

It becomes apparent just how diverse the skills need to be when the nine roles for successful teams, identified by Dr Meredith Belbin, the management guru, are applied to the practice of architecture (see table overleaf). And yet the psychometric profile of students, which will fundamentally determine what roles they will play in an office, is not used as a guide to what educational emphasis may be appropriate for their future careers.

The two years of practice that forms part of the architectural training could and does, help to adjust some of the shortcomings of design-led architectural training. But the transition between education and practice is not facilitated or coordinated by either party. Even though some schools designate a practice tutor to look after the welfare of the students whilst in practice and even though schools seem to charge a fee for the students in their year of practice, the latter arrive at work with nothing but a logbook as their umbilical cord.

Practitioners do not ask the schools what they should do for the students, the schools do not ask what the professionals intend to do for the students and the architectural institution does nothing to encourage such a conversation. The two elements of architectural training are disconnected, just as the content of the education is disconnected from the nature of practice.

There is an urgent need to review architectural education and review those who are teaching it. Maybe in time some new subject matters and some new skills could be embraced by the architectural education system. Meanwhile, the purposeful and talented students who flock to the profession in ever increasing numbers will continue to forge their own paths to meaningful and happy practice and will do so with some help from the exceptional teachers and employers they may be lucky to encounter, as well as their own efforts to unlearn some of the teaching and to find what is missing from their education within society itself.

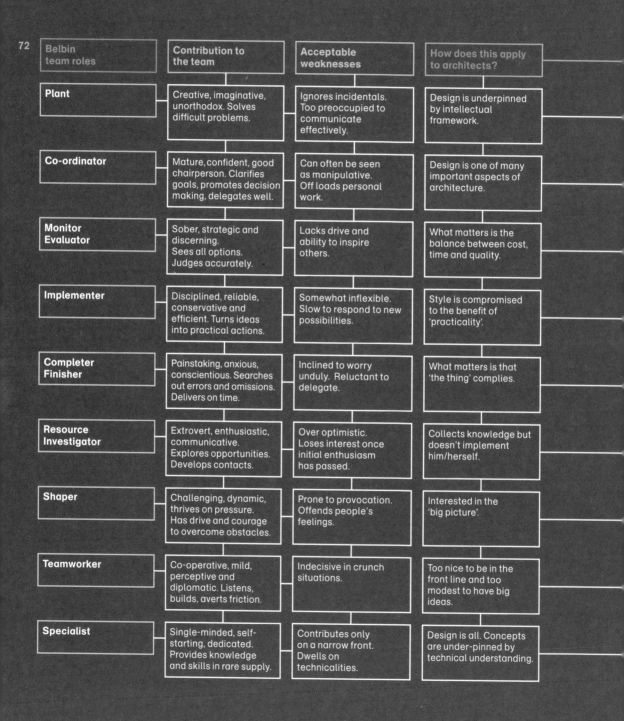

Belbin team roles	Contribution to the team	Acceptable weaknesses	How does this apply to architects?
Plant	Creative, imaginative, unorthodox. Solves difficult problems.	Ignores incidentals. Too preoccupied to communicate effectively.	Design is underpinned by intellectual framework.
Co-ordinator	Mature, confident, good chairperson. Clarifies goals, promotes decision making, delegates well.	Can often be seen as manipulative. Off loads personal work.	Design is one of many important aspects of architecture.
Monitor Evaluator	Sober, strategic and discerning. Sees all options. Judges accurately.	Lacks drive and ability to inspire others.	What matters is the balance between cost, time and quality.
Implementer	Disciplined, reliable, conservative and efficient. Turns ideas into practical actions.	Somewhat inflexible. Slow to respond to new possibilities.	Style is compromised to the benefit of 'practicality'.
Completer Finisher	Painstaking, anxious, conscientious. Searches out errors and omissions. Delivers on time.	Inclined to worry unduly. Reluctant to delegate.	What matters is that 'the thing' complies.
Resource Investigator	Extrovert, enthusiastic, communicative. Explores opportunities. Develops contacts.	Over optimistic. Loses interest once initial enthusiasm has passed.	Collects knowledge but doesn't implement him/herself.
Shaper	Challenging, dynamic, thrives on pressure. Has drive and courage to overcome obstacles.	Prone to provocation. Offends people's feelings.	Interested in the 'big picture'.
Teamworker	Co-operative, mild, perceptive and diplomatic. Listens, builds, averts friction.	Indecisive in crunch situations.	Too nice to be in the front line and too modest to have big ideas.
Specialist	Single-minded, self-starting, dedicated. Provides knowledge and skills in rare supply.	Contributes only on a narrow front. Dwells on technicalities.	Design is all. Concepts are under-pinned by technical understanding.

Can education do justice to all the diverse roles of architects?
Belbin team roles applied to architects

Architectural education does not, at present, sufficiently acknowledge the diversity of architectural contributions likely to be needed in the future.

Frivolous stereotyping What do they do?	Size of the Ego?	Favourite aid	What they'd do with a bonus	Role in garden shed design
Master/guru/young talent waiting to get past the master. More likely to be found in Private Sector but if in Public Sector they are priceless.	Big but discrete due to confidence and pronounced sense of self.	Brain.	Forget they got it.	Suggest flat pack solution.
Business partner in design led or commercial practice. Likely candidate for RIBA Presidency. Chief officer in Public Sector.	Big and aware of it.	Personal Assistant.	Upgrade car and aftershave or perfume.	Pull together Design Team.
Good project manager.	Big but is in denial. Just sulks a lot.	Spreadsheet.	Invest it.	Suggest Design and Build.
Project Architect— second in command or a sole practitioner.	Under control.	CAD.	Home improvement.	Suggest flat roof instead of a pitched one.
Not in any command position but relied on heavily to get it right in the implementation stage.	Too worried to have one.	Manuals.	Put it in the pension scheme.	Check the size of the biggest available mower.
Well suited to the 'portfolio' society likely to do other things such as co-ordinate lecture series or teach part-time.	Big but charming.	Mobile phone and lap top.	Blow it on him or herself.	Research international best practice in shed design.
Principle in private practice. Short term spells in Public Sector.	Big and fragile.	Microphone.	Blow it on others who are but an extension of him or herself.	Get the job and publicise it.
Project Architect.	Perfectly poised.	Tea pot.	Have a nice meal and put the rest in joint bank account.	Draw and write the specification.
Designer. Could be a sole practitioner.	Very fragile. Feels that (s)he is the only one making a contribution.	Pen and paper.	Use it to further his or her knowledge base.	Design it.

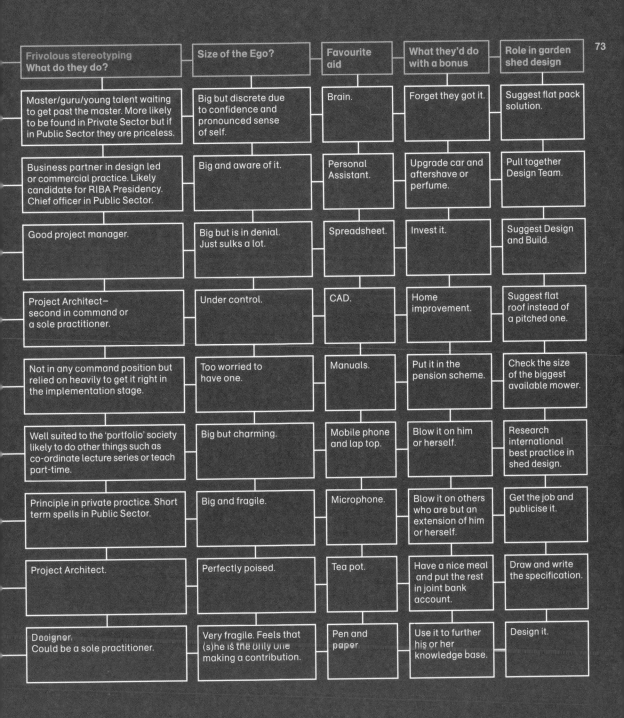

2.1

What architects of the next generation might need to know:

Current architectural education lacks diversity. Architectural practice requires additional skills. Design and creativity are at the heart of architecture but a successful architectural team requires architects with other skills. It's time we accepted this and allow education to diversify.

1 CPD FOR DESIGN TUTORS

3 WHY ARE QUANTITY SURVEYORS USEFUL?

What do Commercial agents do?

plain english

BUSINESS PLANS & BUILDING BRIEFS

2 COMMUNICATION SKILLS

CLIMATE CHANGE

Policies and how they influence building trends

sociology

Surveying Construction Sites

Research Methods

ENVIRONMENTAL BEHAVIOURISM

Iconic Architecture Before & After

4 Design for Sustainability

Why is urban design different from architecture?

negotiation and reconciliation

working with

grumpy communities

LISTENING SKILLS

SKILLS

Possible initiatives to broaden architectural education:

- **Train (the) design teachers.**

- **Recognise different contributions that architects make.**

- **Diversify education to suit choices of architectural roles.**

- **Consider offering:**
  - research methods training
  - integrate environmental sustainability
  - languages
  - working with communities
  - business management including business planning
  - funding
  - leadership
  - conflict resolution
  - construction placements
  - urban design to name but a few

- **Provide cultural exchanges with foreign and home students.**

- **In Part 2 differentiate between preparing chartered designer architects and chartered executive architects. Diversify marking system—less weighting for design in second option.**

- **Integrate professional training into architectural education by having a learning contract for students.**

- **Reinstate apprenticeship system as an alternative to degree.**

I feel coming on a strange disease—humility

Frank Lloyd Wright

We witness a premature declaration of the masterpiece. The consequence is architecture of credit, capitalising on expectations, cashing in on fame, a true phenomenon of the New Economy. When will this bubble burst?

It is not difficult to see how the proposed image of the genius-architect belongs to what remains to architecture today. This image is not endowed with the responsibility to guide us. What is left is a select group of winners-take-all who are doing the most prestigious projects in the world, but are also representing a lost ambition; no longer are architects prepared to respond to the questions: What is important today? What can architecture do to understand this world, to cope with its dynamics, and to intervene? And on top of that: what can architecture as a discipline enact, if architecture as a material order increasingly becomes part of the iconography of hate in the emerging clash of civilisations and its course to urban warfare?

Ole Bouman

There is always a point when one senses one's lack of skill, the doubt.

Arne Jacobsen

Chapter 2.2
Vanity in Architecture:
Disconnections Between
Image and Reality

Disconnections between image and reality have become an acceptable aspect of Western society. The architectural profession has embraced this cultural laziness with enthusiasm. The profession has fallen in love with the surfing culture of sound-bite journalism and is now complicit in its propagation.

Only a few architects can claim to be household names, but the profession has created a stardom system for its own consumption and architecture itself has become a big and sexy media subject.

Unfortunately the coverage of architecture in the national press and journals is rarely found in economic supplements, or in society pages, or in technology and innovation journals. Architecture sits most comfortably on the pages of the lifestyle magazines. Journalists perceive its value and therefore that perceived by the public, to be either a novelty item or a desirable lifestyle accessory.

As the trend-conscious and trend-setting editors of lifestyle magazines, in charge of informing the public of what is a 'must have' for the coming season, set about making their selection, only the most marketable, iconic and seasonal images get through. Once safely sieved through the editorial eye, they are presented as killer images, with a single credit and a very brief commentary designed not to alienate the reader, who is in any case likely to look only at the images and the caption.

This genre of architectural dissemination also affects the world of architectural journalism. The tendency towards vanity in architecture is constantly fuelled by the coalescence of historians, teachers, practitioners and journalists who seem to be in a state of perpetual agreement about what constitutes noteworthy architecture, thus greatly restricting the range of architectural debate. As in any exclusive club, the well-defined entry criteria enable easy identification of those who are admitted and their protection once inside. If there are remnants of the old establishment in the architectural profession, this is where it can be found at its most exposed.

More and more, the relationship between idea and realisation is becoming tentative. While wonderful speculation can be produced, and while the occasional spectacular project is realised, we must not forget the status of normality. What should 'normal' architecture be? What should our efforts add up to?

David Chipperfield

Architecture is a relatively new profession. During the seventeenth century there were only a few architects, and most of them went to Italy. At the same time thousands of houses along the canals of Amsterdam were built almost without architects. This situation persisted until late the late nineteenth century. In the early twentieth century, many architects suddenly appeared, all trying to be original. But the quest for originality doesn't do the architectural profession or the city any good.

Another burdensome paradigm of the twentieth century is the political standpoint of the twentieth century architects—a standpoint that does not recognise and accept the continuity of history. Deep down inside, these architects are restrained by a passion for revolution. This notion, held by those who experienced the1960s, and then by the following generation—unable to take its own stance, but unconsciously following its predecessors—drives them desperately towards the new and the original.

Felix & Kees

2.2

Dissemination of architectural output only as an iconic achievement of one architectural hero requires faithful contributions from all five participants in the architectural establishment:

Teachers, who teach as they were taught, school young architects to aspire to stand out and have their own unique message that will help them on their way to recognition.

The profession provides outlets for these desires through a system of design competitions, 'class of' lists, student awards, and BD's Young Architect of the Year Awards, emphasising a single route to happiness for all young professionals, obscuring other possibilities.

Architectural Journalists happily pick up the stories of work that has been approved by the profession. Awards are then bestowed by the profession on the published buildings. The editors sitting, more often than not, on the awards committee, further reduces the need for critical and intellectual disagreements.

Historians take their cue from the journals as to what architecture needs to be recorded for posterity. This results in further preservation of the professions' unwavering conviction that the handful of iconic designs are more significant than the mass of everyday ones. All steps are further served by an army of highly trained architectural photographers who glorify their subjects to a status of isolated, unoccupied sculptures. The buildings are awarded and photographed on the day, or just before, completion—before the clutter of users spoils the image. And then they are ready for multiple publications.

In search for diversity of debate we reviewed weekly and monthly architectural journals over a 12 month period and what we found was the staggeringly repetitive coverage of award-winning buildings and award-winning architects and over 90 per cent of them from London.

We also found that after publication, neither the judges nor the journalist nor the photographers return to any of the awarded buildings. It was rare for them to seek the opinion of the users to inform their judgements. And they display no interest in the test of time. They were also unwilling to acknowledge that the architectural effort spent on the daily backdrop of a place could have greater relevance to a greater number of people.

In this respect, architecture has shown itself once again ready and willing to embrace the makeover culture, content not to worry its glamourous self with the gritty reality just beneath the surface.

2.2

Educators, journalists, critics, historians and professionals promote a narrow set of values preoccupied with the iconic and one that is inadequate for the challenge ahead.

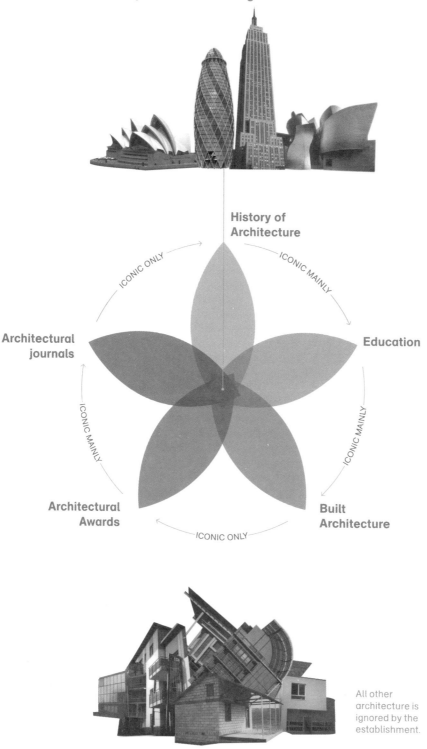

History of Architecture

ICONIC ONLY

ICONIC MAINLY

Architectural journals

Education

ICONIC MAINLY

ICONIC MAINLY

Architectural Awards

Built Architecture

ICONIC ONLY

All other architecture is ignored by the establishment.

2.2

But there is another aspect of the fashion world which could encourage our profession to take a broader look at our collective values. Fashion does recognise what we appear to be ignoring: the mutual dependence of high couture and high street fashion.

It is possible to acknowledge the undisputable value of innovation, originality, technical excellence and stylistic trend-setting in architecture whilst recognising and awarding the equal importance of other values such as extensive availability, cultural relevance, local variations, local ownership, to name but a few. This argument, however, is missing from the current thinking of the British architectural establishment.

This circle of vanity, which is giving rise to headlines such as "Profession out of touch" could be broken by any one of the five petals, but it is not, because the system has a fail-safe way of excluding anybody who does not share the same value system. The profession protects itself in a variety of ways, most notably by persistently failing to engage with the many voices of national newspaper critics and journalists, and members of the general public who often question the dominant values of the profession.

It buries its head in the comforting sand of self-congratulatory rituals instead. The 'old boys' network' has a less defined identity today, but it lives on nevertheless.

To substantiate all these perceptions we reviewed 12 shortlists and commissioned a young journalist, Rosa Silverman, to interview five of the past 12 winners of the RIBA Stirling Prize, the highest accolade in British architecture. Furthermore one of the most common building types, housing, has been nominated only once and has never won. The pioneering low carbon BedZED scheme lost to a high carbon 'iconic' dance school in 2002. The interviews revealed a considerable amount of dissatisfaction among the users of all of the buildings. Most tellingly, some of the problems were fundamental to the point of making the building unsuitable for its purpose.

We are all, as participants in the architectural profession, complicit in sustaining the increasing detachments of the architectural establishment from wider society through our action and even more so our inactions.

We know that single authorship is not possible in architecture but we consent to accolades for single heroes.

2.2

We know nobody can judge one building as being objectively better
than another when each serves a different place and purpose, but
we continue submitting our projects for awards.

We know the public rarely shares an opinion of the professionals,
but we do not take time to investigate why.

We know that questions such as: How sustainable is this design?
Just how flexible is this building? How culturally accessible is it?
Who benefits? would deliver a different selection of award-winning
buildings, but we don't question the current assessment criteria.

We know there are extraordinary designers working on sustainable
neighbourhoods, disaster shelters, better environments in deprived
areas, empowering communities through self-build, new housing
models, new methods of construction and we know this work has
a social value as relevant as, or more so than, the flagship buildings.
We do not ask why the profession regards this work as less worthy of
awards. Worthiness has little appeal in comparison with glamour, but
we do not try to shift the value system underpinning this status quo.

**Our vanity prevents us from looking back and revisiting what we have
done, and it prevents us from abandoning the pursuit of personal
recognition to pursue shared knowledge and wider relevance.**

The perpetuation of a pecking order in architecture based on a
narrow set of values alienates most of the profession from the
rest of society and its members from each other. It denies us the
possibility of realising our full potential as a body of highly trained
analytical problem solvers who are well placed to contribute to
resolving many of the significant problems facing us all today.

**Contemporary British architecture does not have a critical political
voice and we are a profession out of touch with our own potential.**

It will take a new generation of architectural thinkers to move us out
of the iconic image groove and re-focus us on applying our talents
to create places capable of dealing with the enormity of change that
lies ahead of us.

Photographs shot before the RIBA Award (below)
and three years after (bottom).

Photography telling a different story.

Jetty fenced off by Health and Safety Officer.

THIS STRUCTU
A PIECE OF PU
ART NOT
PLAYGROU

EAST RID

2.2

Bridlington before and after:
What happens after the Prizes?

Manipulating reality:
Awards and photography are some of the tools used to fuel
architectural vanity, a process similar to make-overs in
the fashion world.

Tensile fabric destroyed by vandals.   Lack of maintenance.

2.2

Stirling Prizewinners Revisited

In 2006 Bauman Lyons Architects commissioned journalist Rosa Silverman to investigate how clients and users of Stirling award winning buildings feel about their buildings. The research findings confirmed our concerns regarding inadequacy of the award selection process and captured the headlines of national newspapers.

The truth about these iconic buildings: the roofs leak, they're dingy and too hot.
Matt Weaver

Many of the other buildings to scoop the prize have failed to live up to praise heaped on them. Critics say architects have become detached from everyday life and are calling for a rethink of the prize so buildings are judged on how well they stand up to use.

Irena Bauman, a Leeds-based architect and one of the government's design advisers, said architects had become seduced by style over substance.

"Even iconic buildings, as Stirling buildings undoubtedly are, suffer from a host of minor defects which is forgivable. However, some of them are inadequate for their purpose. This is embarrassing for buildings receiving the highest architectural accolade in the UK."

"... Architects are extraordinary problem solvers, [but] instead of engaging with the needs of society we are busy strutting and perpetuating the self-serving image of a profession out of touch with its own potential."

The book's researcher, Rosa Silverman, revisited past winners of the prize and talked to users and those responsible for their maintenance. She writes: "On almost every guided tour I was presented with a long list of faults, which all detracted from the superficial splendour and raised the question of just what the Stirling Prize was actually rewarding."

The Guardian
14 October 2006

2.2

The power of dissemination by journals:

Bauman Lyons Architects commissioned researcher Alison Gillespie to review featured projects in 12 months of publications in 2005–2006. Weekly and monthly architectural journals were reviewed. The key findings indicated a high level of repetition of a small handful of architectural projects.

Architect	Number of times cited	Number of projects featured
Adjaye Associates	4	1
Alison Brookes	3	2
Alsop Architects	6	4
Avanti Architects	3	2
Behnisch & Behnisch & Partner	4	2
David Chipperfield	3	2
Feilden Clegg Bradley	14	11
Foreign Office Architects	5	4
Foster and Partners	4	4
Gareth Hoskins	4	2
Grimshaw	3	3
Herzog and de Meuron	5	4
Jean Nouvel	3	1
Rem Koolhaas	4	4
Renzo Piano	3	2
Richard Reid Associates	3	3
Richard Rogers Partnership	7	4
Snell Associates	3	2
Wilkinson Eyre Architects	5	3
Zaha Hadid	12	5

Top 20 most cited architects

This table lists 20 of the most cited architects (from the articles recorded both in the weekly and monthly journals). The most cited architects are Feilden Clegg and Zaha Hadid.

The table indicates the number of projects featured of each practice listed, in some cases only one project was cited a number of times, for example in the case of Adjaye Associates where the Idea Store Building was featured four times. In other examples i.e. Feilden Clegg, 14 references referred to 11 different projects. As a general trend there does not seem to be a great deal of repetition of architects' projects, (the number of projects cited is quite high in relation to the number of times an architecture firm is cited). Zaha Hadid provides the best exception where only five projects were featured in a total of 12 citations.

Research Undertaken

Journals reviewed:
The Architects Journal (weekly),
Building Design (weekly),
RIBA Journal (monthly),
The Architectural Review (monthly),
Architecture Today (monthly).

34 monthly journals reviewed. 57 weekly journals reviewed. 74% of the monthly journals reviewed contained at least one project article featured in another monthly journal reviewed.

Repetition between journals therefore could be considered high (however only one repeated article in each magazine does allow for many other projects to be featured).

Repetition in the weeklies did not seem to be as high but many of the same projects were featured as in the monthly journals.

Award winners and competition entries were repeatedly featured. Projects featured in advertising increased the perception of repetition.

There were very few examples of projects at construction stage in the monthly journals–there were more in the weeklies by way of news articles and repeated features.

The presentation of most feature articles was very standard providing internal and external photography and plans and section drawings.

Geographical distribution of projects featured was wide.

2.2

The cult of the 'single creator' is perpetuated by iconic images of the creator of iconic building.

Ernö Goldfinger at Trellick Tower, Cheltenham Estate, Edenham Street, North Kensington, London.

Furthermore, when a global culture has no unifying faith, the iconic buildings will continue to prosper, perhaps even increase in volume. We might then step back from reaction and learn to understand the new genre.

We might distinguish a few superlative creations from the more numerous failures, for the best work… shows the basic temper of the times and, as Ruskin said, judges its character. The iconic building, when successful, puts architecture on a par with the best contemporary art to explore freely the possibilities of open-ended creativity.

Jencks on celebrity architecture from *The Iconic Building* by Charles Jencks.
Vicious circle of vanity perpetuated by one of its creators.

Provocation:

In today's design paradise, there is a desire, as never before, for cutting edge architecture. The architect has become a media star and architecture, a spectacle. The public demand for newness, excitement, monumentality, 'culture', pleasure, safety, memory and other cosmopolitan trends has created a new kind of arms race with design as the crucial weapon.

With the happy integration of Architecture in our culture, the question as to the architect's place in society becomes all the more urgent. Most projects seem to appease rather than define a more ideological position; to promote the culture industry, rather than challenge the wonderland of late capitalism.

But our world is undergoing explosive and rapid changes: the old political, technical, and social lexicon of space has become obsolete. On the one hand, our civilisation — through further deregulation, migration individualisation, corporate globalism, imperialism, expansion of technology and media, environmental abuse, and economic warfare — is collapsing.

Can the architect project alternatives that deal with the urgent questions and issues of our civilisation? What should Architecture do today and what shouldn't it do? In other words: What is an Architect in today's society?
Roemer van Toorn

3.0

Chapter 3
Four Ways of Practising Architecture
Architects' Choice

Architects, just as every other profession, are in a permanent state of impermanence; they are also, unlike many other professions exposed to ever more rapid tidal waves of fashion. Roemer Van Toorn has posed a question with which our team has been wrestling over 15 years of practice.

In previous chapters we examined the concept of disconnections, which we are proposing architects are well placed to stitch as our contribution to the making of a better society. We considered the multiple disconnections caused by rapid rate of change of the context of the architectural practice, and the disconnection appearing within the ever more complex client bodies. We also identified some of the many disconnections, which are impacting on the making of our cities. We reviewed the disconnections between education and practice and the ever increasing tendency to disconnect image from reality, a practice borrowed from life-style magazines by architectural journalism to encourage the already excessive vanity of the architectural profession, ultimately sustained by a proliferation of architectural awards dished out by architects to themselves.

We all, as a profession, seem to accept this status quo without a challenge. We appear satisfied with a handful of iconic images as representative of our contribution to the built environment. And we remain silent on the subject of why so many of us are prepared to produce ill-considered buildings and places that don't work often spending much energy on blaming everybody including the client, lack of money, planners, project managers, users, and the system—everybody but ourselves. We are as uncritical of our individual work as we are of ourselves as a profession.

The context of a society in a increasing state of disconnections combined with total lack of effort from the architectural fraternity to harness our considerable intellectual power and creativity towards a concerted effort to stitch these gaping disconnections of wealth and poverty, life-style and climate change, need for beauty and the reality of blandness, finally leads us to ask the questions:

Are architects powerless to engage with such issues? Are we beholden to various masters who impede us from doing so, or do we have a choice?

What is an architect in today's society? The increasing pragmatism of today's architectural discipline is going nowhere because architects are not trained to take control of that process; instead, they have become an instrument of the common market, controlled by political autocracies and building pragmatics. In this sense, architecture today is an impotent discipline. Instead of pragmatics only, architects should again be concerned with defining the everyday problems of ordinary people and finding solutions to them!

Mika Cimolini

3.0

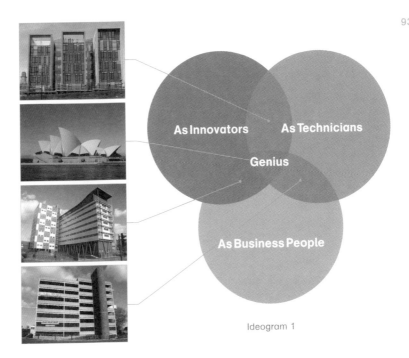

Ideogram 1

Four Types of Product

There are four ways of practising architecture: predominantly as businessman, as technician, as innovator and as a genius who can be all three.

'Predominantly Businessman' are architects who practise architecture in order to make money. Architecture itself is just the means to an end.

'Predominantly Technicians' are architects who are preoccupied with satisfying purely technical functions, such as making the building stand up and making it watertight.

'Predominantly Innovators' are design architects who are preoccupied with problem solving in terms of design solutions, the procurement and the social context of architectural work.

'Predominantly Genius' is the architect who can do it all and do it well. (Ideogram 1)

It is not possible to produce architecture unless there is an overlap between two predominant aspects of practice—the extent of the overlap determines the type of output created.

3.0

Four Ways of Practising Architecture

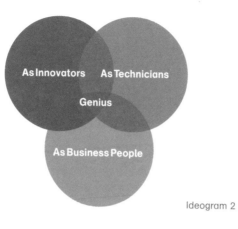

As Innovators As Technicians
Genius
As Business People

Ideogram 2

What is each type of architect likely to be doing?

Design and Social
Architecture

Health and Safety

As Innovators As Technicians

Commercial
Architecture

Genius

Thinker Academic
Historian Critic

As Business People

Property
Development

Specialist

Ideogram 3

Four Ways of Being a Client

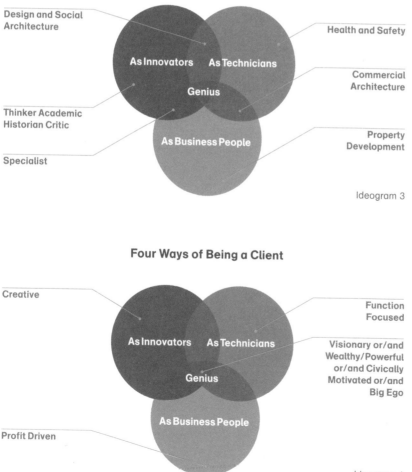

Creative

Function
Focused

As Innovators As Technicians

Visionary or/and
Wealthy/Powerful
or/and Civically
Motivated or/and
Big Ego

Genius

As Business People

Profit Driven

Ideogram 4

3.0

Businessmen alone cannot design or build without either technical or innovative input. Likewise, technicians need the business or innovation aspect to build just as innovators needs either business or technical support to translate ideas into buildings. (Ideogram 2)

This simple model can be applied to clients (Ideogram 3) and the types of architectural output. (Ideogram 4) It is a dynamic model—the extent of overlap can vary and the three circles are spinning plates prone to be influenced by external forces and kept in balance by the architectural team.

The model can be used to explain certain patterns in architectural practice. For example, young practices who make their name as good designers quite often loose their design excellence in the process of successful expansion as they move from innovator/ technician to technician/businessman model. Those who become commercially successful whilst retaining a strong innovation base become geniuses.

The choice of how we practise defines our clients and our output —it is as unlikely for a commercial architectural practice to produce groundbreaking buildings or attract a client who wants one, as it is for an innovative design led practice to land a major commercial client. All students are thought to be innovators but most of them become technicians and businessmen in the process of practice.

Most of recorded, published and taught architecture is produced by the handful of genius' of architecture—whilst the contributions of others who are responsible for the vast majority of the built environment are less considered and discussed, let alone awarded.

We have always hoped to practice as innovators and technicians. This does not mean that we are not viable commercially—only that commercial success is a secondary consideration. Using our creativity to design good buildings, to realign faulty processes and to mend disconnection is where our happiness in architectural practice resides.

Where are you on the ideogram?
Is this where you want to be?

To the teachers who inspired us. To all our clients who trusted us with their wonderful projects. To all the collaborators who contribute their skills, knowledge and creativity. To all our staff who have brought so much talent to the team. Thank you for 15 years of fulfilment.

Maurice, Lillian, Guy, Simon and Irena

4.0

The most difficult of misalignments to manage in practice is that between the desire to practise in an ethical way and the nature of available work combined with the need to be a commercially viable business. We have managed this disconnection by working locally and keeping the team sufficiently small to allow a bespoke response to each project. In a buoyant economy this allowed us to turn down unsuitable projects. In a less buoyant economy this approach allowed us to survive in business.

All our projects, despite their diversity, share one common trait: they involve the stitching of disconnections. These come in many disguises: disconnections that occur on the edges of physically separated neighbourhoods, economically excluded communities, culturally isolated clusters, marginal economies, marginalised activities, inappropriate procurement processes, inadequate policies and lack of skill, power and commitment to the future.

To help stitch these into a meaningful story, we had to review some of the ways of thinking we were taught in schools of architecture, acquire some new skills which we were not taught at all, expand the skills in the team beyond traditional architectural practice and get to know the places where we are working so that we can guide our clients wisely. To illustrate some of these points we have selected some projects and grouped them by the nature of their edge condition:

The Edge of New Technologies
The People at the Edge
The Edge of Viability
The Edge Between Nature and the Man-made
The Edge of what we know.

They represent our recurring interest in architecture being a tool for connecting the marginal to the mainstream.

Local

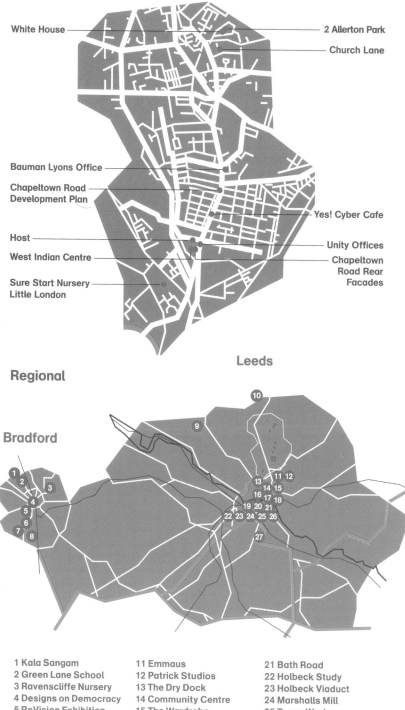

White House — 2 Allerton Park

Church Lane

Bauman Lyons Office

Chapeltown Road
Development Plan

Yes! Cyber Cafe

Host

Unity Offices

West Indian Centre

Chapeltown
Road Rear
Facades

Sure Start Nursery
Little London

Leeds

Regional

Bradford

1 Kala Sangam
2 Green Lane School
3 Ravenscliffe Nursery
4 Designs on Democracy
5 ReVision Exhibition
6 Reyner House
7 Bus Shelters
8 Woodroyd Centre
9 Spandler House
10 North Parade

11 Emmaus
12 Patrick Studios
13 The Dry Dock
14 Community Centre
15 The Wardrobe
16 The Calls
17 Holdforth Court
18 Malthouse
19 Hepworth Chambers
20 Dark Arches

21 Bath Road
22 Holbeck Study
23 Holbeck Viaduct
24 Marshalls Mill
25 Tower Works
26 Holbeck Pavilion
27 Clarence Dock

Mapping 15 years of
projects reveals a cluster
of work within two hours
of travel from the office.
Working in this way allows
better knowledge of the
place, better service to the
client, better life-style for
the design team and
lighter eco-footprint.

28 Garston
29 Cleckheaton Town Hall
30 Arts Council Reception, Dewsbury
31 Batley Town Hall
32 Dewsbury Town Hall
33 The Media Centre
34 Ollo
35 Southern Extension
36 Yorkshire Sculpture Park
37 Barnsley Digital Media Centre
38 Shirecliffe Community & Childrens Centre
39 York Art Gallery
40 Arc Light
41 South Promenade, Bridlington
42 The Terrace Cultural Quarter
43 Carlsberg Brewery, Copenhagen

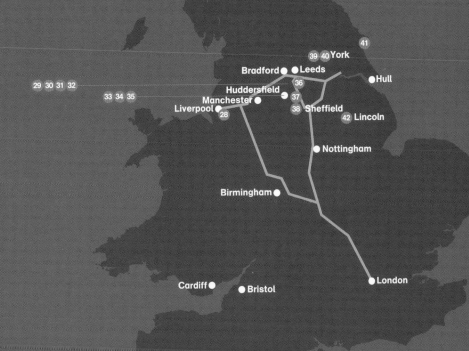

Copenhagen 43

Edinburgh

Newcastle

41

39 40 York

Bradford ● ● Leeds

Hull

36

29 30 31 32

Huddersfield

33 34 35

37

Manchester

38 Sheffield

Liverpool

28

42 Lincoln

Nottingham

Birmingham

London

Cardiff

Bristol

If you give people tools, and they use their natural ability and their curiosity, they will develop things in ways that surprise you very much beyond what you might have expected.

Bill Gates

It is not the strongest of the species that survive, nor the most intelligent, but the one most responsive to change.

Charles Darwin

Bauman Lyons Projects
The Edge of New Technologies

Creative and media centres are emerging all over the north of England.
Two reasons can be given for this. First, they can be a catalyst for
regeneration in a community like Chapeltown which had untapped
creative and media potential. Secondly, an increasing number of
young people are being educated in our towns and cities at expanding
universities. This is true for creative and media courses, but many
graduates are lured away to London. By developing regional media
centres cities, can retain the talent they educated and grow their
creative industries economy.

Since 2000 BLA have been involved in this new typology starting
with two refurbishment projects; Host Media Centre, Leeds and The
Media Centre, Huddersfield. Recent projects in Barnsley and Lincoln
show a growth in scale as the typology has become established by
proving itself successful.

"Creative and media centres are multi-occupancy buildings that
provide offices, studios and facilities for small companies working
within the creative industries sector. These buildings are managed
so as to aggregate costs and services so that small creative firms
can benefit from reduced overheads and added value services, as
well as collaborate and share skills, both of which significantly allow
their long term sustainability."

Toby Hyam, Client Director of Creative Space Management

Host
Leeds Media Centre

At Host, Leeds' first media centre in the often maligned area of Chapeltown, an unlovely 1920s building last used as a club for the trade union movement and originally as a centre for the Jewish community, has been re-built into a facility for local musicians and start up media companies.

A cocktail of funding from the regional development authority, City Council, sponsorship and Lottery money enabled the project to happen. The project was driven at grass roots level by the community's desire to help nurture the wealth of local musicians and media companies. Successful regeneration, to our mind, has to have a social significance of this kind.

A poor quality 1970s addition to the east end of the building was demolished in order to create an opportunity for a striking piece of contemporary architecture expressing the difference between old and new, signalling the new cultural activity from Chapeltown Road and housing the larger volume recording studios which could not be accommodated within the old structure.

BLA have been involved in ten projects along the one mile long Chapeltown Road corridor and have been instrumental in developing a masterplan framework for the regeneration of Chapeltown.

In 2007 we built and moved into our own offices on Chapeltown Road, the first private sector commercial office investment in the area for over 70 years.

Black Building, our office

Yes! Cyber cafe (2002)

Northern School of
Contemporary Dance
(extended by Allen Tod
Architects)

Host, Leeds
Media Centre

Unity Housing Association

West Indian Centre
refurbishment
and landscaping

Rear of Chapeltown Road
Facade Improvements

Other Architects
Bauman Lyons Projects

Right: View of the entrance area and new extension housing the double-height film studio and signalling the new facility to Chapeltown Road.

Below: Successful media centres provide a variety of informal and incidental spaces for conversation and meeting. The balcony at Host provides one such space by which these interactions are encouraged.

Middle: One of the recording studios.

Bottom: Chapeltown Road Redevelopment Plan community consultation held at Host in 2006.

The Media Centre
Huddersfield

Huddersfield is a large mill town with a Victorian industrial past. It is conveniently situated between Leeds and Manchester with excellent road and rail access and is surrounded by beautiful countryside. The town is attractive to aspiring city dwellers who cannot yet afford the lifestyle of the cities. It was recognised that there was a growing demand for workspace from small media and creative companies in the area.

The second phase of the development, the conversion of a warehouse in the town centre was designed into a managed workspace for 30 creative and media companies. The derelict building was carefully repaired and given a new identity through the insertion of an entrance and stairwell element.

View of the refurbished building and new entrance created from reconfiguring an existing shopfront.

The building was almost beyond repair when the project started in 1999. The new structural central core provided the stability of the building without disturbing or having to upgrade the foundations of the existing walls.

An ongoing working relationship with the Media Centre led to a number of commissions. The refurbishment of the cafe to form Cafe Ollo (right) was completed during summer 2005. The success of the project was the degree to which the space was transformed within a period of only five weeks.

The Terrace Cultural Quarter
Lincoln

Lincoln gives the impression of being a well-healed picturesque cathedral city, and yet is predominantly working class. It is surprising that the University opened its doors for the first time in 1996.

The Terrace provides continuity in encouraging the comparatively recent and growing young pool of media and creative talent to stay in Lincoln and contribute to the diversification and strength of the local economy.

The project is located on the social/economic edge between fine artists, craftsmen and creative industry businesses and the physical edge of the old Medieval city and the modern commercial and retail centre.

The character of the Flaxengate area and the long alley ways plots running along the contours of the hill generated our proposal to split the large facility into three separate buildings linked at high level. We have aimed in the design to continue the Medieval tradition of high proximity, high density, permeability and the possibility of being surprised. The shallow depth of the buildings allows good daylight penetration and natural ventilation. The model demonstrates how the mass was broken into three distinct buildings which are varied in height to mediate between the buildings of Medieval scale rising up the hill in the background and the modern city in the foreground. This was one of the first buildings to demonstrate to us the successful synthesis of historic forms to create highly sustainable buildings.

Left: model of the scheme in context.

Bottom left: Tenant Ted Brewer, violin maker in his studio.

Bottom right: Ground floor occupied by jeweller Elizabeth Rowlett.

Digital Media Centre
Barnsley

114 Alsop Architects' Re-making Barnsley–
Strategic Development Framework received
love/hate reviews on publication in 2003. Our
project is one of the first major developments
in Barnsley's regeneration. The building is
a symbol of the future, heralding a new era in
the city's life. The project intends to achieve
an environmentally and socially sustainable
development. To do this we have considered
the needs of particular forms of construction
and the building's users, in conjunction with
the ambition of creating a landmark quality
building. It is these considerations that have
generated an environment rather than just a
building. The building form is broken into three
elements linked with one atrium. This achieves
many design objectives:

- Avoids the negative impact of a large
singlemass and creates a 'cluster' rather
then an 'institutional' image.
Creates permeability through the building.
- A 'Connector', rather than an 'Obstacle'
to movement through the city.
- Offers natural ventilation and daylight
throughout the building.
- Provides clear orientation throughout
the building.
- Generates excellent communal spaces
where most of the informal communication
takes place.
- Creates a sustainable building form that
offers options for conversion and multiple
ownerships in years to come.

In our concept visual for the competition (left) we sought to bridge the gap between a realistic physical expression and the conceptual imagery of the adopted vision for Barnsley.

The design stayed completely true to the original design concept but evolved through considerations of the realities of context, materials and construction (right). We found it surprising how important a role this image played in enthusing everyone involved in the process from client to site operative.

Panoramic view looking west.

Continuity of Vernacular Materials

We chose stone as the main external material. It is contextual and sustainable and enabled us to explore different textures with one material. The ashlar stone provides the perfect canvas for the play of light at sunset. The gabion walls at the base ground the building, respond to the rough hewn stone of the existing retaining wall and gives texture and relief at ground level.

Innovation

We developed a series of mesh shutters to control solar gain on the southern elevation and a system to get the metal mesh to look like frozen fabric. Originally we intended to use bronze, but that would eventually fatigue due to wind buffeting. Instead we used stainless steel and heat-treated it to reach the desired colour. The mesh cuts out 50 per cent of the light incident on the glass but is relatively transparent and also gives softness to the external elevation.

Below: A silver bracelet belonging to one of the architects, was the inspiration for the building's external shutters.

Near left: A close up of the building showing the composition of tactile materials

Left: View toward the main entrance from the lower le

Top: View along
County way.

Bottom: An open roof-
top room on the top floor
adjacent to the conference
room with a superb framed
view looking east across
the valley.

Developing New Sustainable Forms

Traditionally office buildings require a four metre floor-to-floor
height due to the depth of concealed ceilings and floors required
for the provision of services. By forming shallow floor plates we
are able to avoid these raised floors by distributing the power and
data around the perimeter and naturally ventilating the space.
The floor-to-floor height is then reduced to 3.4 metres economising
on the building's volume. The shallow floor plates enable the
building to be ventilated naturally from windows in the external
facade, through sound attenuated louvers above the doors, to
louvres in the atrium roof.

Views of the many
different people involved
in the project, from
tenants to contractors,
to some of the guests
at the opening event.

The building's occupation will be phased over a three year period.
As the centre gains tenants the central atrium will become the social
heart of the building. Nearly every tenant unit has a threshold to this
space where wide balconies provide space for the informal interactions
that are essential in creating a dynamic creative industries hub.

The site occupies a commanding position in Barnsley in both prospect and aspect. The prospect is a magnificent view afforded of Barnsley valley due to the terracing of the slope, a legacy of the previous use of the site as the Courthouse Station and the topology of the land steeply sloping away to the east. The aspect of the site is a key reason for the location of the building on the new Courthouse Campus. Its proximity to the new transport interchange and the view from the railway line enable the building to have a strong visual presence, necessary for promoting the businesses it hopes to nurture and support.

The most important resource for the future of a city... is the knowledge, ingenuity, and organisational capacity of citizens themselves.
Anonymous

The more you can increase fear of drugs and crime, welfare mothers, immigrants and aliens, the more you control all the people.
Noam Chomsky

Some believe there is nothing one man or one woman can do against the enormous army of the world's ills—against misery, against ignorance, or injustice and violence. Yet many of the world's great movements, of thought and action, have flowed from the work of a single person.
RF Kennedy

Bauman Lyons Projects
People at the Edge

Throughout our work we perceive that disconnection in the physical fabric of towns and cities is reflected in the disconnections between different economic and ethnic sectors of our society.

The marginalised areas of cities more often than not house the marginalised people. It is this condition that is often misunderstood when regeneration is equated with gentrification and all marginal uses that contribute to the making of a democratic city are wiped out and in the process sanitise the regenerated area into protected clusters of the privileged minorities.

The marginalised sectors are varied; the poor, the ethnically different, the economically unviable, the old, the young, the infirm, the artists... the list goes on. In many of our projects we have explored how different marginalised groups can be accommodated in those marginalised locations and observed how powerful a regenerator this can be for both urban fabric and the people who inhabit it. Our role on such projects expands beyond the role of an architect into facilitation, consultation, mediation, dissemination and championing. The architectural ego has no part to play.

Funding for all of the projects in this section was so limited that only the bare essentials to make the buildings habitable, safe and functional were achieved. And yet it could be argued that the social value of these projects reflects the achievements of a civilised society as much if not more then a flagship award-winning commercial or cultural project. Who is it that is ultimately responsible for determining the architectural value system that elevates one effort higher than the other?

Emmaus Leeds
Burmantofts

124 Emmaus Communities offer homeless people a home, work and the chance to rebuild their lives in a supportive environment. There are currently 14 Communities around the UK and several more in development. They rely on donations of furniture and household goods from the public. The companions, who reside on the top floor, repair the goods on the lower floor workshops and sell them in the Emmaus shop on the ground floor.

The site, a large old school building, was made available to house the homeless project by the church owners who were prepared to forego higher profits offered by the private sector developers.

Everybody who was involved in the project from the previous owners of the building, the board of trustees to the smallest supplier gave something beyond the expected so that the budget stretched to deliver what should have been a £2 million project for £1 million on a city centre site. Emmaus satisfies many homeless people's needs in providing a home, work and the chance of a new life.

The Emmaus concept is an extraordinary example of a sustainable way of life, and the architecture responds to this. The scheme is economic, logical and focuses on the issues of spiritual needs relating to identity, privacy and a sense of worth. Projects like Emmaus are only made possible by such a convergence of will, which connects strands of society, economy and the city that usually are disconnected.

Emmaus

'The crime bridge' Allegedly a third of all Leeds City Centre Crime is facilitated by this bridge in the view of a local police officer

The inner city ring road

Patrick Studios

Quarry House Government
Department of Health,
Department of Work and Pensions

Emmaus is about people, many of whom arrive at Emmaus at a very low point in their lives. People become homeless for many different reasons, but relationship breakdown, bereavement, addiction or abuse have often played a part. In Emmaus they find the space and support they need to start rebuilding their lives.

These people come from a wide variety of backgrounds and all bring different skills and experience to Emmaus. What brings us together is our shared commitment to enabling those who have been homeless and excluded from society to rebuild their lives and help others. The central values of Emmaus, shared by the worldwide Movement, are set out in Emmaus' Universal Manifesto.
Emmaus

Patrick Studios
Burmantofts, Leeds

Restored Patrick Studios.

Patrick Studios, a £1,500,000 refurbishment project, is the outcome of two artists inspirationally toiling for years in a city with little interest in the visual arts to finally secure studio space and support facilities for the city's artists. Without any previous experience of capital fundraising, capital projects or project management, they succeeded in overcoming every possible hurdle to deliver the studios over a three year period.

As with the Emmaus project, the building was only made available because of the site owners' preference for a marginalised user and their understanding of the cultural benefits to the city of building art studios rather than yet another commercial or residential development. The East Street Arts, with Patrick Studios as their base, now sustain an art programme that has spread its influence wide into the city and is helping to change perceptions of art within the public realm and the city's consciousness.

Below: The second floor studio was created by inserting a box within the building volume. It is set back from the external walls creating a top-lit open plan studio and part double-height studios to the floors below ensuring that the new floor does not cross in front of the original windows.

Top: The new facilities at Patrick Studios have enabled East Street Arts to successfully promote Situation Leeds; an independent contemporary visual art festival, bringing together artists and arts organisations to explore art in public places through installations, events, debates, video and publications.

Bottom: Patrick Studios community of artists.

Opposite: The large volume of the Project Space enables exhibitions, talks, gatherings and the production and display of large-scale art works.

SECOND CHANCE FOR CITY HOSTEL

By Richard Waite

On 16 August 2005, a man thrust a baby into the face of Arc Light project director Jeremy Jones, and accused him of wanting to kill his son.

The incident was indicative of the heated reactions that followed an open day for local residents to discuss plans for a controversial new hostel for the homeless in Clifton, York.

Homeless charity Arc Light wanted to build a £3.5 million, 34-bed homeless centre – designed by Leeds-based practice Bauman Lyons – in a former secondary school as a replacement for the organisation's existing, rather Dickensian, city-centre hostel.

Part of the government's £90 million Hostels Capital Improvement Programme, the innovative scheme looked likely to be the first flagship project to make it off the ground.

Yet the anti-hostel clamour from concerned locals and, more importantly, from local politicians, was so great that Jones felt he had no choice but to withdraw the application, pulled on 30 September 2005.

Now, almost two years later, Bauman Lyons is about to begin on site with Arc Light's all-new hostel proposals (pictured) – a remarkable turnaround for the project, the charity and the practice.

The new £3.4 million building – the Centre for Change – will also provide accommodation for 34 people, plus a café, training rooms and the charity's offices.

However, unlike the original Shipton Street proposals, this three-storey brick building will not sit among York's Victorian terraces. Instead it will occupy the north-west corner of the city-centre Union Terrace car park – a design challenge in itself.

The car-park plot was one of more than 30 sites considered by Jones and city planners after the demise of the initial project.

Fundamental to the success of the second attempt was the 'opening up' of the tricky selection process and the securing of cross-party backing for the proposals. As a result, the application passed through the planning process almost unchallenged, except for a bizarre discussion over potential drainage issues.

Jones, a retired rock-band manager, said: 'The day after the open day [for the first scheme] was the only day in seven years of developing Arc Light that I wondered whether we would ever be able to change people's minds.

'The second time around, a public announcement of cross-party political support and a broad and transparent public consultation during the site selection stage went a long way towards minimising the risk of failure.'

Jones is convinced that the design of the new building will accelerate the process of helping the homeless to take that next step towards permanent resettlement. He says: 'The building overlooks the former Bootham Park mental hospital at the rear. This Classical, quasi-Palladian façade hides what is going on behind.

'Our apparently random fenestration [towards the car park] reflects that all sorts is going on here... The recessed windows which point to the city show we are truly part of the city too.'

**Second Chance
for City Hostel**
Richard Waite

Architects' Journal
April 2007

On 16 August 2005, a man thrust a baby into the face of Arc Light project director Jeremy Jones, and accused him of wanting to kill his son. The incident was indicative of the heated reactions that followed an open day for local residents to discuss plans for a controversial new hostel for the homeless in Clifton, York. Homeless charity Arc Light wanted to build a £3.5 million, 34 bed homeless centre—designed by Leeds based practice Bauman Lyons—in a former secondary school as a replacement for the organisation's existing, rather Dickensian, city centre hostel.

Part of the government's £90 million Hostels Capital Improvement Programme, the innovative scheme looked likely to be the first flagship project to make it off the ground. Yet the anti-hostel clamour from concerned locals and, more importantly, from local politicians, was so great that Jones felt he had no choice but to withdraw the application, pulled on 30 September 2005. Now, almost two years later, Bauman Lyons is about to begin on site with Arc Light's all-new hostel proposals (pictured)—a remarkable turnaround for the project, the charity and the practice.

The new £3.4 million building—the Centre for Change will also provide accommodation for 34 people, plus a cafe, training rooms and the charity's offices. However, unlike the original Shipton Street proposals, this three-storey brick building will not sit among York's Victorian terraces.

Instead it will occupy the northwest corner of the city centre Union Terrace car park—a design challenge in itself. The car park plot was one of 30 sites considered by Jones and city planners after the demise of the initial project. Fundamental to the success of the second attempt was the 'opening up' of the tricky selection process and the securing of cross-party backing for the proposals.

As a result, the application passed through the planning process almost unchallenged, except for a bizarre discussion over potential drainage issues. Jones, a retired rock band manager, said "The day after the open day [for the first scheme] was the only day in seven years of developing Arc Light that I wondered if we would be able to change people's minds. The second time around, a public announcement of cross- party political support and a broad and transparent public consultation during the site selection stage went a long way towards minimising the risk of failure." Jones is convinced that the design of the new building will accelerate the process of helping the homeless 'to take that next step' towards permanent resettlement. He says: "The building overlooks the former Bootham Park mental hospital at the rear. This Classical, quasi-Palladian façade hides what is going on behind. Our apparently random fenestration [towards the car park] reflects that all sorts is going on here....

The recessed windows, which point to the city, show we are truly part of that city too."

Above: Arc Light photograph of Jacko as he is now and as he appeared in an Arc Light leaflet while living rough.

ARC LIGHT

when love is Unconditional

love counts.

I used to sit outside Bettys playing the penny whistle. Now, with the help of Arc Light, I desperately want to try to sort myself out. I have stopped begging, cleaned myself up and want to make a go of having my own flat. With enough support I won't mess it up. I know how much there is to lose.

Jacko

Sure Start Nursery
Little London

A modest project in the heart of Little London, one of the most deprived neighbourhoods in the centre of Leeds. The building, designed to reflect the traditional way children draw houses, provides a pre-school nursery for up to 60 children with crèche facilities and community support services.

Despite its location in an area known for vandalism problems, the building has not been subject to vandalism.

Parents were involved in the selection of the architects, in brief writing and design reviews. It was the parents who refused to accept our proposal for an all slate clad building and insisted on mixing the slate with timber. The process of ongoing consultation created a sense of ownership and increased confidence of those involved in their own judgement. The building has become a lively focus of community activities and a source of local pride.

I did tests on small stones before collecting and committing myself to the larger ones.

I soon realised that what had happened on a small scale cannot necessarily be repeated on a larger scale.

Andy Goldsworthy

Bauman Lyons Projects
The Edge of Viability

Small projects for clients who want something very special but have a restricted budget to fulfil their aspirations are potentially commercially disastrous but creatively very rewarding.

These projects are most likely to provide training opportunities for students and young architects. They allow the job architect to experience the full process from conception to completion in a relatively short time and offer direct contact with client, other consultants in the design team and the builders, sub-contractors and suppliers.

In these projects architects can only provide a good service if any disconnection between their aspirations and those of the client are acknowledged and resolved from the outset.

The skill of diplomacy becomes the most valuable asset as the architect often finds herself/himself in the midst of marital disputes, confessionals and stressful environments, all of which require skillful mending.

Spandler House
Leeds

Rather than move, the client wanted to extend their 1940s semi-detached to include a family room and graphic design office. The new extension orientates the double-height family room to views to the south and large glazed openings make connections with the garden.

Daylight washes down the existing external wall that is now enveloped into the house through a continuous roof light. A balcony overlooks the double-height space from the studio at first floor. The materials are predominantly glass, render and plywood, all simply detailed.

Southern House
Huddersfield

"We knew that we wanted to create a light, modern and beautiful space for cooking and socialising without disturbing the traditional building that has been in the family since it was built. What we didn't expect was that opening the corner of the house to the sun and the garden would change the way that we live in such a dramatic way.

The surroundings make eating healthily and exercising into enjoyable activities. Now we're convinced that, like Pal for dogs, it'll prolong our active lives."

Stuart Nolan and Jen Southern
July 2006

Marshalls Mill
Holbeck, Leeds

Marshalls Mill reception forms part of a 6,500 m² Grade 2* listed mill built in 1815. It was acquired by Igloo Regeneration in 2003 for a mixed-use redevelopment that would positively contribute to Holbeck Urban Village.

Bauman Lyons were approached to improve the character and the functionality of the existing ground floor reception area.

The refurbishment aims to provide a benchmark for future development. The scheme is aesthetically and spatially contrasting to the existing while being sympathetic to the original character of the mill.

Arts Council Reception
Dewsbury

The existing reception area was dark, uninviting and had a poor relationship to the street. By redesigning the fire exit from the building, the old solid lobby that acted as a barrier to the openness of the space, could be removed and be replaced by a small glass inner lobby.

New interventions were then placed in the cleared space to reorganise and create more successful relationships. New windows were added to the gable wall to flood the space with light. Ceilings and flooring help to define the routes within the building.

Issues of accessibility and inclusivity were design generators and not appended features once the concept was complete.

North Parade
Leeds

The client lives in a five bedroom Edwardian home in the northern suburbs of Leeds. The house lacked a sense of connection to the garden, the sunniest section of which was occupied by an old garage.

The brief was to relocate the garage to the north-facing driveway and create a new space that formed an enclosure but became an extension of the garden. The decision was taken early on in the design's evolution to build a separate garden room rather than create an extension. Care was taken in detailing and use of materials to ensure that the transition from the traditional street aspect to the contemporary rear aspect was sensitive and appropriate.

Church Lane
Leeds

The clients wanted a new extension that was beautifully designed and crafted. These requirements evolved through discussion—a room to eat and entertain in to create an intimate and private space, which mediates between the house and the garden.

This was achieved through using a combination of the existing load-bearing structure (from the demolition of a previous extension), building new rendered block work walls, adding the timber monolith warm roof and timber sliding doors.

No house should ever be on a hill or on anything.
It should be of the hill. Belonging to it. Hill and house
should live together each the happier for the other.

Study nature, love nature, stay close to nature.
It will never fail you.

Frank Lloyd Wright

Bauman Lyons Projects
The Edge of Man-made and Nature

The majority of our projects are built within the context of a man-made environment. In such projects our design decisions are guided by considerations of good urban design and successful place-making.

A small selection of our projects are located within the context of nature that challenged us with a new set of design considerations. Man has not been very successful at responding to the extraordinary condition of the sea edge as evidenced by the 3,400 miles of coastline in England. More often than not we have simply continued the urban language right up to the edge of the sea, neither recognising nor acknowledging the beauty of nature and the spirituality of the horizon. Often we have done even worse by turning the edge between nature and the man-made into a fairground.

It is not within the gift of many architects to be able to replicate the shear beauty of nature. We do, however, have skills of control that nature does not have, such as repetition, symmetry, formal composition, geometric massing and juxtaposition of colour.

These are powerful tools with which we can enhance nature when vernacular response of 'being of the landscape' is no longer possible due to changes in social expectations and economic imperatives.

South Promenade
Bridlington

In the early years of our practice, which coincided with the severe recession of the early 90s, we were working hand to mouth with a team of six motivated and optimistic people enjoying the excitement of the smallest of projects.

In 1994 came the crunch and we ran out of work.

Initially we busied ourselves pursuing our deep interest in a neglected industrial area in Leeds known as Holbeck, by energising a large team of stakeholders including the City and a group of artists and musicians in engaging with the future of the area and by raising funds from various sources to stage an exhibition.

This activity did not bring us work then but did set a process in motion which ten years later brought us a number of significant projects.

As a team high in ideas but close to commercial demise was the state in which we received a career changing phone call from a client wishing to commission a feasibility study of the refurbishment of Bridlington South Foreshore. The invitation came on the back of the collaborative work we have done with artists on two small projects on which we paid for the artist fees ourselves because we felt that this would benefit the project and the client.

Thus began our first major project and collaboration with the artist Bruce McLean, which put an end to our first encounter with the edge of viability and marked the beginnings of our interest in the edge between nature and the man-made.

Traditional man-made treatment of the sea edge.

Repetition and colour. Some of the man-
made elements that can enhance nature.

Yorkshire Sculpture Park
Bretton

Yorkshire Sculpture Park was established in 1977 at Bretton, near Wakefield. Longside, on the edge of the park, are three renovated agricultural barns forming a gallery and units for creative industry.

The only retained element of the barns was the portal frames. On a summer's day during construction these resembled whale skeletons. The new designs considered the huge scale of the barns and the landscape. Each new element of the building was scaled up in response. Enormous windows, large doors and elongated ironmongery.

Internally, huge windows frame the horizontal landscape and rise to the sky bringing the scale of the landscape into the barn. Finishes are brusque, a reflection on budget and the former agricultural use.

The architect must be a prophet... a prophet in the true sense of the term... if he can't see at least ten years ahead don't call him an architect.
Frank Lloyd Wright

We always overestimate the change that will occur in the next two years and underestimate the change that will occur in the next ten.
Bill Gates

If you think mitigated climate change is expensive, try unmitigated climate change.
Dr Richard Gammon

The twentieth century was about getting around. The twenty-first century will be about staying in a place worth staying in.
James Kunstler

Bauman Lyons Projects
The Edge of What We Know... the Future

As the rate of change in all aspects of our lives continues to increase, we have less certainty that the decisions we make now will be the right ones in years to come.

This uncertainty is further increased by the growing understanding of the magnitude of change that will be required to modify and adopt our environment and behaviour in response to the challenge of climate change.

As architects we have an opportunity and a responsibility, to build the future in a sustainable way. But in order to do so we need to be knowledgeable and in the vanguard of understanding of the drivers of change and the science and the social needs that underpin them.

We have been challenged through a number of recent commissions to predict and embrace the forthcoming changes and to offer an insight into how we are likely to live and work in the next 25 to 50 years.

Our winning competition entry for a £45 million mixed-use low carbon scheme at Tower Works Leeds, limited competition entry for the 34 hectare Carlsberg Brewery site in Copenhagen and the study into the future of Market Towns in England are some of the recent projects that encouraged us to research and imagine the future and shape it in a robust and responsible fashion.

Tower Works
Leeds

The Tower Works project in Holbeck was won in a national developer /architect design-led competition. At £45 million it was five times bigger than any other job we have previously undertaken. Our phone call, after a supportive tip off, to the developer ISIS, who submitted an expression of interest to bid without a design team on board, was the most important proactive step we took in the 15 years of the practice. Tower Works is one of the most interesting sites on the south side of the River Aire in central Leeds.

The site steeped in industrial history and distinguished by three chimneys, built as Italianesque towers by ambitious nineteenth century industrialists. The towers are visible by train-passengers approaching Leeds from the south. The competition ran by the Regional Development Agency Yorkshire Forward, called for a commercially viable exemplar of sustainable mixed-use urban development that tackles the issues of Climate Change and provides a learning 'log' for others.

Our scheme is based on a number of sound design principles that can be applied to all places but are flexible so that they can be modified to respond to the individual context.
Those principles include:

- East to west orientation of residential blocks.
- North to south orientation of commercial blocks.
- North to south saw tooth roofs to facilitate solar panels, photovoltaics and north lights.
- Maximum depth of any building 14 metres to facilitate natural daylight and ventilation.
- Narrow streets between buildings four to nine metres, to shade and create urban density.
- Masonry high thermal capacity, long life commercial lower floors.
- Timber frame/SIP construction for residential upper floors to facilitated modification in the future.
- Lower floor-to-floor heights through the omission of raised floors and suspended ceilings made redundant because of the shallow footprint.
- Combined Heat and Power plant on site.
- No car parking on site.
- An Italian bakery and microbrewery as the focal facilities to create animation on the main square and a new provision for the area.
- Facilities management of cycle hire, car share and recycling.

The project will take six years to complete in two phases.

It could be argued that we are living through a time when the fundamental values and institutions of society change. Some argue this happens every 250 years or so in the west, exactly the amount of time which has passed since the Enlightenment. What needs to be done to understand these changes and ensure that we develop the capacity in our people, institutions, policies and cultures which help us remain robust in times of such change and uncertainty.

Unknown

Market Towns
The Future

After gruelling written submissions exploring every part of our work, thinking and achievements, followed up by an interview presentation based on a three volume brief received one hour earlier, we succeeded in being accepted onto an exclusive panel of lead consultants for Yorkshire Forward Renaissance Market Towns, a regeneration development agency.

Being on a panel does not guarantee projects and selected consultants need to compete further against each other for each project that is commissioned. However, we were fortunate to be trusted with the most interesting project of them all: a study of the future of Market Towns. It was one of the most engaging pieces of work we have carried out to date.

There are 223 Market Towns in Yorkshire and they face different futures depending on their geographic position, economy, landscape and population. The literature on futures is abundant. Every government department has a horizon-scanning programme and futurologists are springing up all over the place. Most of the work is, however, focused on cities, and we found surprisingly little research on smaller towns.

Identifying the key drivers of change was equally challenging since human beings are notoriously unable to imagine unfamiliar possibilities and in all our projections of the future we tend to default back into what we know.

Nevertheless we accepted seven main drivers of change: climate change, more technological innovation, hardcore of deprivation will persist, ageing population will increase, young adults will continue to be educated in cities, new arrivals are to be expected of environmental as well as economic refugees and interdependence between cities and the city region will continue to be strengthened.

We have identified seven future scenarios which are based on different levels of policy intervention and have examined the spatial implications of change in each scenario. Each scenario has been tested against the characteristics of seven existing towns to ensure that the projected futures are realistic although exaggerated in order to provoke debate.

Each scenario is further illustrated by a diary of the future resident so as to make these futures tangible. It is within our gift, as a society, to create better futures and increasingly a more civilised society, but it is equally in our gift to destroy all we have achieved.

Old Sandcastle
Costal Shrinkage

This is sea edge scenario which is likely to happen if there is no policy intervention.

Location:	Seaside town.
Morphology:	Low-rise, low-density declining town with local centre.
Identity:	Strong sense of working class history. Declining glory.
Population mix:	Ageing, poor white. Only those who cannot afford to leave and have nowhere else to go remain. Largely the most elderly and infirm. They have no insurance and suffer severe depravation. Housing market failure creates cheap housing for environmental refugees who set up extensive camps.
Housing:	Mainly nineteenth to mid-twentieth century terraces and semi detached houses. No new buildings. Market failure due to frequent sea surges and decline of tourism.
Function:	Retirement for the low-income pensioners. Declining tourism destination for the traditional white working class.
Economy:	Holiday homes and service industry.
Transport:	Poor public transport and poor road access. No investment.
Food:	Processed, cheapest available.
Climate Change:	No investment in flood defences. Sea rises and claims the edge of the town.

Policy changes required to avoid this scenario:
- Commitment to building of sea defences.
- Combined with investment in transport links.
- Resourses set aside for remedial work after successive flood damage.
- New insurance products.
- Incentives to encourage tourism expansion on the coast to take advantage of warmer weather and create new economy.

Existing

Future

1. Sea advance and coastal erosion
2. Town abandoned and turned
   into a refugee camp

New Dale
Transformational Society

This is a scenario for a market town which is shrinking due to a decline in traditional industries but re-invented as a town for the future.

Location:	Likely to emerge on the back of the shrinking town.
Morphology:	New energy and CO_2 neutral architecture, medium to high-density with visible energy centres, water retention systems and multi-functional green spaces including cultivation of bio fuel and food. Cellars, food larders, ice houses make a come back and green houses, poly tunnels, retention ponds and winter gardens are common features. Warmer weather encourages social interaction and frequent gales and flash floods require window shutters and stronger structure.
Identity:	Dynamic, progressive and international.
Housing:	Great variety of tenure including housing co-operatives, self-build, collective ownership of assets and profits. Housing used as a perk to the right kind of skill.
Function:	Experimental settlements spearheading the new transformational society. Often built around a specific area of research such as nano-technologies, genetic engineering or information technologies.
Economy:	Largely self-sufficient in terms of energy, water and food. Knowledge based industries. Centres of excellence and learning at research level. Hot Housing Campus for grown-ups.
Transport:	Improved twice a day service to the nearest city. Discrete multi-storey parking facilities on the edge of the town. Electric vehicles only inside the town. Good electric minibus services to settlements in the hinterland.
Food:	Locally grown. Garden and Farmers markets. Special foods ordered on the Internet.
Climate Change:	Controlled through design and investment.

Policy changes required to avoid this scenario:
- Investment in higher education.
- Investment in public transport.
- Decentralised decision-making and support for different forms of governance.
- Investment in new economies.

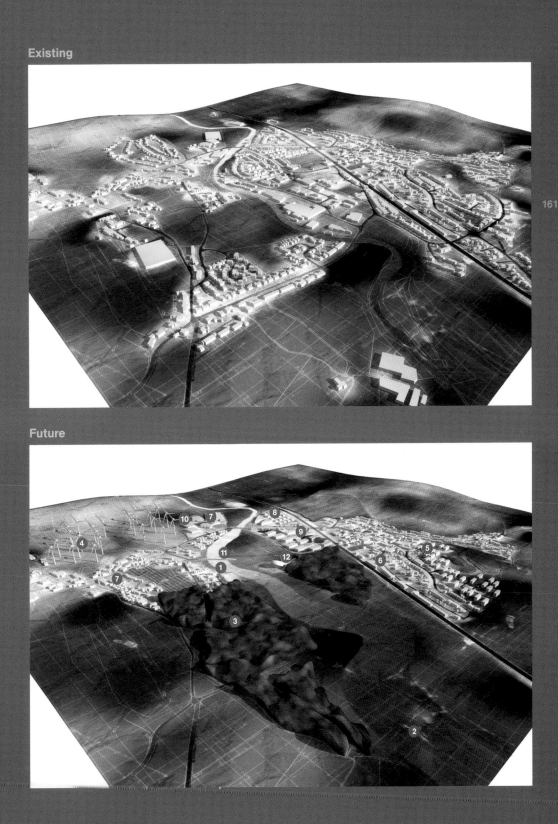

Future

1. Flood defence
2. Wider river
3. Loss of traditional industry
4. New energy industry
5. New eco-neighbourhood
6. Improved station
7. New self-build housing
8. Outdoor pursuit college
9. Enterprise centre for food genetics
10. Exchange warehouse run by people over 70
11. Kyoto Bridge
12. New debating chamber

New Sandcastle
British Riviera

This is seaside scenario likely to happen if there is significant policy intervention.

Location:	Seaside town.
Morphology:	Low density nineteenth to twentieth century architecture but rapidly developing into Mediterranean style holiday resort as result of climate change which brings with it warm weather and decline in foreign travel.
Identity:	Sense of history gives way to complete make over.
Population mix:	Ageing and wealthy middle class.
Housing:	Mainly owner-occupier and expensive but affordable housing protected for key and service workers. New developments are mainly hotels, holiday villages and cliff top villas. Some sheltered luxury apartments serviced by attached enhanced health facilities as well as up market care homes.
Function:	Leisure destination, retirement and employment centre. Conference centre out of season. Holiday business is no longer seasonal with popularity of shorter but more frequent breaks continuing. The resort is for middle-income population and is very multi-cultural.
Economy:	Holiday homes and service industry.
Transport:	Improved service to all core cities and improved regional network. Discrete multi-storey parking facilities on the edge of the town. Electric vehicles only inside the town. Good electric minibus services to settlements in the hinterland.
Food:	Small scale production for tourism consumption and market garden for local consumption. Local fish dishes regarded as desirable unique offer.
Climate Change:	Investment in flood defences. Global warming offers re-invention. Investment in renewable energy and future proofing against further extremes of weather.

Policies required to achieve this scenario:
- Investment in economy.
- Investment in public transport.
- Heavy taxes on flights.
- Investment in sea defences.

Existing

Future

1. Sea defences
2. Improved station
3. High-rise hotels
4. Holiday village
5. Second phase hotels
6. High street
7. Apartments for rent
8. Retirement homes
9. Holiday villas
10. Conference and golf centre
11. Wind turbines
12. Waste recycling

New Meadow
Sprawl

This is a scenario for a desirable market town close to our city where market places are restrained and growth is uncontrolled.

Location:	Likely to be close to a settlement larger than 20,000 population.
Morphology:	Mixture of all forms of housing and architecture. Low to medium density. Number of neighbourhood centres and out of town retail and leisure centres. Transport interchanges.
Identity:	Dispersed neighbourhoods. Separation between workplace and private life. No collective identity but some neighbourhood based civic initiatives.
Population mix:	Mixed with dominance of families. Large influx of newcomers from Europe and environmental refuges. Social tensions alongside new cultural influences.
Function:	Commuter dormitories.
Economy:	Limited economic base made up of service industry and some office and manufacturing for relocating businesses. Growth of distribution centres.
Transport:	Car dependency with main flow to the cities and counter flow of service workers who can't afford to live in the Rurbs. Improved road infrastructure with staggered working hours to cope with congestion.
Food:	Monopoly of supermarkets continues. Consumption levels continue.
Climate Change:	Problems escalate–the wealthy invest in air conditioning, storm shutters and insurance. The less wealthy suffer.

Policies required to prevent this scenario:

- Restrictive planning policies to prevent sprawl.
- Congestion charges.
- Carbon taxes.
- Investment in public transport.
- Restrictive policies on out of town shopping.

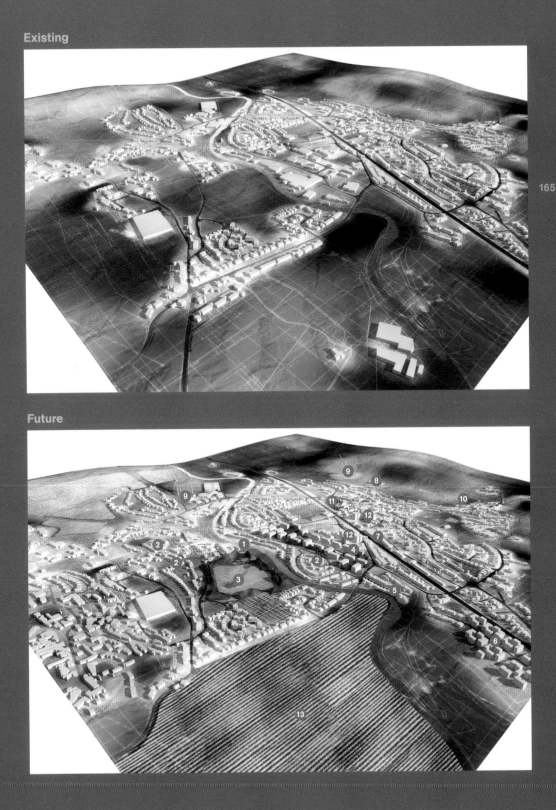

Future

1. Flood defence
2. New housing
3. Leisure park and orchard
4. Business park
5. More housing
6. More affordable housing
7. Improved station
8. Private villas
9. Local wind turbines
10. Underground car park
11. Orchard
12. Commercial development
13. Bio-fuel

Carlsberg Brewery
Copenhagen

In 2003 an international competition was held to design an urban high-density mixed-use scheme in the north of Manchester. It was an ideas competition intended to encourage architects to start thinking seriously about energy use in the built environment. The words "climate change" did not feature even once in the brief four years ago; it did not yet enter the collective consciousness and sustainability was still a vaguely understood concept. We entered the competition, as the opportunity for our team to start learning what we knew was vital for us to know.

This is the best reason for doing competitions. Without the work and the learning we did for this one, we would not have stood a chance, have had the confidence to accept an invitation to the limited international competition for the 34 hectare Carlsberg Brewery site in Copenhagen.

City Rim Study
Leeds

Our first chance to work on a city scale was through a commission from the newly formed Leeds Renaissance Partnership, a board of key decision-makers from the city and two regeneration agencies whose aim was to introduce strategic city wide thinking to determine the direction of growth for the booming city.

This joint work with the City Architect became a year of exploration of the most enigmatic and the least considered two kilometre 'rim' surrounding the wealthy centre of Leeds and separating it from the residential suburbs.

We explored on foot, on buses, in all weathers, through photographs, in history books, in patterns of industry, in patterns of neighbourhoods, in topography and in future flood patterns. We recorded wasteland, green land and places of worship, neighbourhood centres, marginal industries and disconnections by road infrastructure, railways, poverty and fear. We obtained information on current planning applications, patterns of walking to work, conservation area boundaries and most importantly the ownerships of land. We recorded our investigation of this part of the city by taking it apart in 30 layers of mapped information to allow understanding to emerge.

What we found was an intensely interesting part of the city containing everything that other parts of the city did not have including city wide facilities such as universities and hospitals, disconnected neighbourhoods with strong communities, manufacturing and trading as well as neglect, poverty and despair.

Out of this analysis, which would be relevant to all provincial cities, we have developed an influential proposal to connect the rim to the city centre with a sequence of green spaces for leisure, education but also for food cultivation, to create a compact city core fit for the challenges of climate change and able to compete in the global market by offering high standards of living and by tackling the isolation of its disadvantaged population.

The knowledge we have gained and the understanding of the city confirmed what we already believed in; that architects can make the most significant contribution by knowing and working in the place where they live.

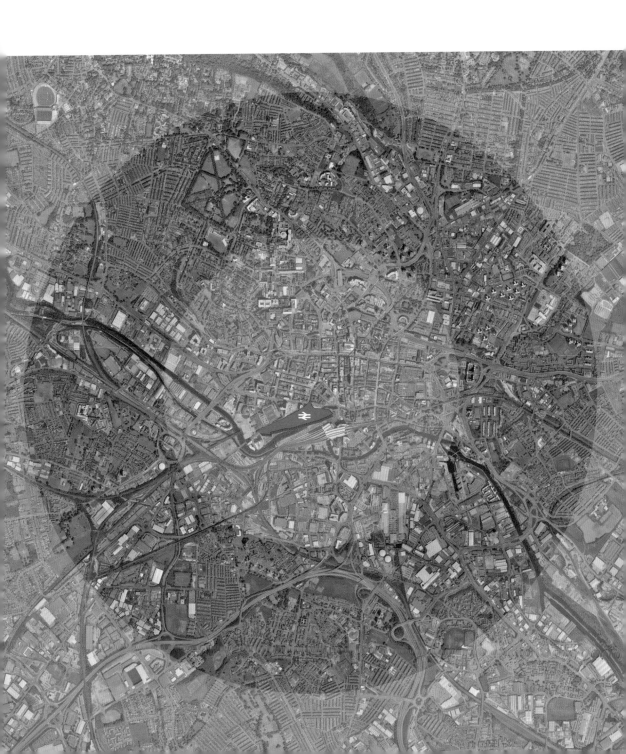

Layers of Mapping Research

170

Waterways

Routes: transport networks

Disconnections

Flood risk

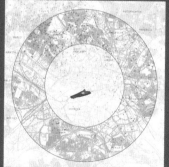
Walk to work

Planning applications

Development pressure points

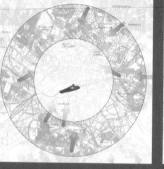
Viewpoints

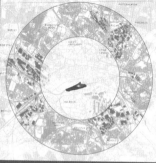
Clusters of employment

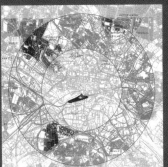

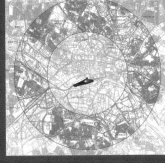

Connected neighbourhoods

Isolated neighbourhoods

City-wide facilities

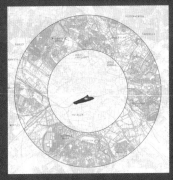

Neighbourhood facilities

UDP green spaces

Green spaces

Proposed green connections

Car parks

Ownership

In many modern cities, a direct connection to the land that supplies them with food or forest products, has all but ceased. Long distance food supplies are becoming the norm. The same is true for water supplies. But as cities extract water for themselves, they often deprive local rural communities of water supplies further contributing to rural-urban migration.

Herbert Girardet, *Cities People Planet*

For the first time in human history, people are systematically building, meaningless places.

EV Walter

Bauman Lyons Projects
Connecting the Edges

The rapid growth of cities, the globalisation of the economy, the shift from citizen to consumer, the rapid changes of policy, the decline of democratic involvement, the growing gap in wealth distribution, the changing patterns of demographics of life-styles are some of the trends that leave their mark on the physical fabric of the built environment.

One such mark is the disconnection between communities and sometimes whole sections of towns and cities.

We have explored a range of different types of disconnections in chapter 1.3. We have arrived at our perceptions through observing the difficulties we have encountered in delivering of infrastructure projects carried out in the last few years.

Difficulties of other types often compound the difficulties of stitching such physical connections: land ownerships, silo structures of stakeholder organisations, inadequate political support; insufficient funding, uncoordinated policies, wasteful procurement methods and inadequate time scales are all familiar barriers.

In this section we illustrate our efforts to bridge the physical disconnections whilst recognising and addressing other barriers to connected cities.

Some of the most important connections are created as an apology to the construction of a new disconnection: railway underpasses and highway pedestrian bridges are common examples.

The Neville Street underpass located under the main Leeds train station platforms also happens to be the main gateway into the city centre from the south. 21,000 pedestrians cross this space every day, crushed alongside four lanes of traffic and bus stops. The space is dirty, noisy, wind blown and cold. As the south of Leeds boomed the private sector employers settling into their new offices demanded a more pleasant connection to the city centre on the north side of the railway tracks.

The challenges of improving such a space are considerable. The bridge is owned by Network Rail who are focused on keeping trains running. As an organisation they are impenetrable and unaware of the potential they have to make other civic contributions by working in partnership with the city. The road is owned by the Highways Department and under the road run several layers of utilities services. Network Rail does not allow anything to be fixed to their structure nor do they want to spend any money on unessential works such as decorations.

Highways have height restrictions, lane width restrictions and a restricted range of approved materials. Utilities companies have a monopoly and are untouchable. We have worked within these tight restrictions and developed a groundbreaking design that incorporates perforated sandwich panels with poured insulation that will alter the acoustics of the space.

On the west side we have worked with graphic designer Andy Edwards and APW Perforators on a moiré effect installation and on the east side with artist Hans Peter Kuhn and LED supplier Solar on a light installation. Hans Peter has also composed a sound installation and in collaboration with ARUP Acoustics developed a permanent sound infrastructure for the underpass. This project could not have been delivered without the constant support of the two project managers who have guided the project through four years of technical innovation and problem solving.

Holbeck
Leeds

The disused viaduct runs across a number of neighbourhoods to the south of the city centre, crosses the Leeds to Liverpool canal and connects to the train station at its northern end.

The Viaduct is currently a barrier between these neighbourhoods. The masterplan to regenerate an old industrial area into Holbeck Urban Village identified its potential to create a connector.

There are already examples of such projects, most notably the Highline in New York and the Viaduc des Arts in Paris. It is proposed that Leeds establishes a linear park on top of the Viaduct as part of the city's wider strategy to create a walkable, green city in preparation of the behavioural and social changes ahead.

Ideas developed with Estell Warren Landscape Architects exploring a green route which retains qualities of a rail track but enhances the landscape to emphasise seasonal changes and vary the experience of the landscape along its length by establishing a gradient of controlled man-made landscape at the northern city through to a wild natural landscape at the far end to the south.

178

Bus stops are, arguably, the smallest possible democratic structures. They are also practical and everyday.

Many clients have perceived their potential to contribute to the identity of a place and to make an iconic splash. Bradford City commissioned six bus stops on the back of their investment into a new rapid bus route system to celebrate the significant investment in the future of the city.

The commission was won in a limited design competition in collaboration with Forced Entertainment artist group and Greyworld sound artists. The average design team meeting consisted of 20 or so people: bus operator's engineers, bus operator's bosses, health and safety officers for the council and health and safety officers for the bus route provider, access officers, branding consultants, funders, politicians, client representatives, contractors for the bus route, design team... to name but a few. The range and multitude of restricted design codes, rules and stipulations reflected the complexity of the client group.

The process appeared totally out of scale with the project. Every aspect of design had to be justified and presented in a convincing manner—every departure form the 'norm' was questioned. The bus stops, have heated seats powered by a wind charger and ingenious art installations and although controversial at the time, have not been vandalised in the five years since they have been constructed.

Bauman Lyons Office
Leeds

We have built our office to fulfil many of our dreams: to be our own client, to have a tailor made work environment, to stop paying rent and to use our investment to assist with the regeneration of a vibrant but troubled inner city area of Chapeltown in Leeds. We are the first commercial office building in Chapeltown in the last 70 to 80 years.

The new office has also allowed us to start making adjustments in response to the challenges presented by climate change. We use less energy, compost and recycle our waste, walk and cycle to work more, as many of our team have moved into the area and we have space to grow vegetables, herbs and flowers.

As we write this book and look out of the window from the first floor studio we can still see a car park full of cars. We have begun the uncomfortable process of changing our energy rich life-styles but still have a long way to go.

It is not possible to practise architecture alone. The breadth of required knowledge and the range of necessary skills make team work the condition of architectural practice.

In this book we have taken a critical stance on the repetitive practice found in our profession of crediting architectural output with a single name. However, this is not to say, as we have pointed out in Chapter 2.1, that there is no role for leadership within a team. Quite the opposite: all teams need to be led but this is often misrepresented as single authorship.

Our team has grown from three to 23. Within this growth the lead team has grown from two to five. And yet the practice ethos has not changed since its inception and the team, although constantly changing, has always embraced the ethos rather than alter it.

It is the ethos of the practice that stitches the team together. The key role of architectural partners, directors and principals is the establishment of such an ethos—they are the ones responsible for which clients are sought out, what values are imparted in the design process and ultimately, for the standard of architecture the practice produces.

The ethos that seems to have stitched our team throughout the 15 years of practice, as captured in the individual revelations of our team members contained on the following pages is the appreciation that architecture is creative, challenging, exciting and above all socially purposeful when at its best.

5.0

What Gets Us Out of Bed?

Alison Gillespie
Researcher

Anna Ulak
Architectural
Assistant

Beth Riley
Architectural
Assistant

Chris Carter
IT Systems Manager

I have to be honest; I find it quite hard to get out of bed in the morning. This morning my alarm was set for 7.32am. I turned it off. In fact, I turned it off at least three times and eventually dragged myself out of bed at 8.12am.

My difficulty with getting out of bed doesn't stem from dissatisfaction with my work; I enjoy the challenge of balancing my work, university and social life. It is simply that I associate my bed with warmth, relaxation, privacy; and companionship four of the most enjoyable experiences of each day.

My dreams are what get me up in the morning... ok, a bit of a one liner but its true... I dream about my past, my future, my family, my friends...

For me the morning is all about the power of nature. The warmth of the sun through my window draws me outside in order to feel nature at work. When you feel something as powerful as the sun rising how can you not want to expose yourself to as many instances of the natural world asking you to work alongside it. Experiences such as these constantly remind us that we are living as part of a complex relationship between ourselves and the powerful environments that we inhabit. It is impossible to feel anything other than an acute awareness of our humble importance as individuals in the presence of such surroundings. This sensation, which strikes me as integral to the continual development of our relationship with our environments, informs my personal approach to architecture; an architecture that is considerate, responsive, interactive and, most importantly, humble.

I'm not a morning person. I'm definitely a night owl who's always last to leave the party. Bed is somewhere to recharge my batteries. For most people seeing 6am on the clock means it's time to get up - for me it usually means I've stayed up a bit too late.

Walking in the Dales at dawn when the wildlife is most active and the frost is still on the ground never ceases to amaze me. The only thing as beautiful is my daughter.

One thing I really look forward to is my drive to work. I'm a bit of a petrol head and there's nothing better than the adrenaline rush of a powerful car to wake me up.

I could do 90% of my job from a laptop in bed but reward comes from working with friends, implementing cutting-edge technology and seeing how it improves people's lives.

As I get older I realise just how short life is and how valuable my time is on this small rock hurtling through space. I just have a different idea of when to enjoy my time than most.

5.0

Guy Smith
Architect

Irena Bauman
Architect

Issa Bensalem
Architect

Jem Taylor
Architect

No man ever said on his deathbed, "I wish I had spent more time at the office."
Senator Paul Tsongas

Since we spend 50 per cent of our adult lives at work, this seems a sad and wholly unsuccessful censure on the choices we make in living our lives.

Through privilege of upbringing and education I have the freedom to make choices. I am fortunate. I have chosen to make my passion my career. It takes comparatively little effort to drag myself from the comforts of a warm bed for the chance of spending the day with people I like, doing things that inspire and challenge me and that I enjoy and that seems to me a sound choice.

That's on good days. But some mornings I am more taken with the words of WC Fields; "Start every day with a smile and get it over with!"

"Getting out of bed in the morning is an act of false confidence."
Jules Feiffer

However, if at the end of the day you get into bed having spent it creatively with people you like, producing relevant work, learning and being challenged, drinking good coffee, getting paid for it, having a laugh and sharing that bed with the person who had a similar kind of day, then the confidence has been vindicated. And if your children want to be like you, this is the best you can wish for and as good as it can possibly get.

"We have a lot of choices. If getting out of bed in the morning is a chore and you're not smiling on a regular basis, try another choice."
Steven D Woodhull

I could not ask for more than for my work to be something I would like to be doing anyway, even if I were not being paid. Architecture satisfies the desire to achieve and create something out of the ordinary, useful and beautiful and provides some pleasure and satisfaction along the way.

"Don't you know that most people take most things because that's what's given them and they have no opinion whatever?

"Do you wish to be guided by what they expect you to think they think, or by your own judgement?"
Ayn Rand
The Fountainhead

Oh yes, joy—new day! Rub sleep from eyes, carve bristles from face, hot water, soap, dry, clothes, slug back coffee, get on down to work. No, not just work—but architecture. You know—designing and creating spaces, buildings and stuff. Stuff being: arguing with contractors, writing schedules and more stuff.

I'm still influenced by things from my student days like: "architecture is not a career, it's a lifestyle" and the edict of the architect as grand creator, such as Howard Roark in Ayn Rand's novel *The Fountainhead.*

This can lead to a bit of an unbalanced approach. The key for me is to enjoy all the other stuff as well—climbing a big hill, fresh air, see new places and learn new things—then I enjoy architecture all the more. That gets me out of bed.

5.0

Jonathan Davis
Architect

Lee Holmes
Architect

Lillian Allen
Practice Manager

Mark Bailey
IT Systems Manager

Nothing. Everything. Someone. Something. It changes every day. But I'm reluctant to get up, because lying in bed is a perfect place to think—I think about the day and what I can achieve, think about the past and how it led me here and think about my plans for next week or next year. Some of my best ideas arrive when I'm in bed—the trick is remembering them. And when this small piece of the jigsaw has been slotted into place, I'll start the day. Unless I'm hungry for a bowl of Alpen and some coffee and then the jigsaw of life can wait.

What gets me out of bed, and more importantly into the office daily [and often at weekends] is a passion for my chosen profession. Working with similarly minded and driven individuals forming a team, that pretensions aside, are producing something of worth and hopefully with a social conscience.

BLA see and are an active part/influence on the wider horizon and I'm learning a great deal daily about the profession and practice of architecture in an inspirational environment. Having studied for nearly nine years, having found a practice that sits well with my own sensibilities, having a sense of achievement and job satisfaction, that is what gets me and keeps getting me out of bed.

Life itself gets me out of bed, that feeling of amazement and veneration for what each new day may bring. My Mum used to always say "you get what you give", so each day I try to live life to the full and give to it as much as possible and my Mum was right, I reap the benefits in so many different ways!

I am a bit of an insomniac and definitely a night owl so sometimes it is hard to know when one day ends and another begins. The morning can come as a bit of a shock, but the physical act of getting out of bed is expedited by having two young boys to feed.

Once I am up and active, the mental act of getting out of bed soon kicks in and before too long I am anxious to get out the door to explore thoughts and ideas I had the night before.

Having the type of work that also happens to be my hobby means I am immersed in technology twenty four seven and there is not a day that goes by where a new product or development is announced that requires research and comprehension about how it fits into the larger picture. This provides a varied, intellectual and fulfiling role that I would not swap for anything in the world.

Unless of course that 'thing' involves a beach and a fishing rod…

5.0

Mat Best
Architectural
Assistant

Matt Murphy
Architectural
Assistant

Matthew Slinn
Architectural
Assistant

Maurice Lyons
Architect

"Everything will be all right in the morning."

The waking brings with it all the wonders of nature, from the colour of the morning sky, to humanity's commitment to finding answers in a fluctuating world. It brings with it opportunities to right your wrongs, to acknowledge our short falls and act upon these. Everyday is a challenge with no winners or contestants, just a chance for us to plot on "our" charts what we would like to achieve.

"I wake to sleep, and take my waking slow I learn by going where I have to go."
Theodore Roethke
The Waking

I hope I continue to wake for many years to come, to see the effects of life upon my face, I may not recognise the face I see. But by looking beyond the wrinkles, the effects of failures and sorrow, joy and happiness, I am sure I'll be looking back at the real me.

I don't know why but for me there are two very different answers:
If I have somewhere to be then I will probably hit the alarm as many times as possible whilst weighing up in my head how I may be able to reduce the morning routine so as to afford a few more precious moments of peace and warmth! I would say what gets me out of bed in this case is mostly self discipline, although its not as though I don't want to get up, I appreciate how lucky I am.

However, if the day is my own I will usually be out of bed early and I enjoy it, I like to seize the moment and get the most out of my own time, I feel more and more guilty the longer I stay in bed but I am usually inspired by something to get me going before that happens. In this case what gets me out of bed can be anything from a beautiful sunrise to a single thought or idea, but more than likely it will be something that will get me closer to where I want to go in life.

With all the routines we impose on our lives, one may come to expect that every day will be the same. This is never the case. Expect the unexpected. Be it an action, comment or experience, the smallest instance can change a mood quite considerably. I live for those moments that make your day, the ones which when recalled make you uncontrollably smile to yourself on a busy street. These special interactions with the people, places or things you love just somehow make it all worthwhile.

Why is it, I ask myself, that I manage to retain the enthusiasm to get out of bed each morning at 6.00am to go into the office early.

One reason is to get as many hours at work each day as possible to enjoy the interesting work along with the attendant learning and understanding that each day brings. Each day is a challenge that repeatedly reminds you that you "know nothing".

The thought that a lot of people depend on my input before they can carry out their work is a powerful reason not to linger in bed. Whether they are in-house or external consultants, the consequences of ones own non-performance causing delay is a powerful get-out-of-bed device.

However, the most potent reason for leaving the bed in the morning has to be the responsibility of running the business in the first place, with all the individuals who depend on its health. The thought of letting them down is too horrible to keep me in that nice warm bed.

5.0

Rachel Codling
Graphic Designer

Sam Wilson
Architect

Sascha Seberina
Architect

Simon Warren
Architect

Being loud. Being quiet. Thinking. Not thinking. Dancing. Sitting. Silence. Music. Watching. Being watched. Playing. Being toyed with. Singing. Being serenaded. Missing. Being missed. Variety. Routine. Work. Play.

My brother and best friend both tell me they hate Sundays: they spend the whole day dreading Monday. I rarely suffer this kind of pre-work torment. At the beginning of the week – even if I know it's going to be frantic as hell – I never think that it won't be worthwhile. I get up at some ungodly hour, beat the rush and sit in an (almost) empty office, enjoying the quiet and planning my day. I write lists (all kinds of lists, I'm a compulsive list maker, I have a colossal list open on my desktop right now with everything I could possibly need to do in the next three months of my life), I make a big pot of black tar for me and the other bleary-eyed early birds and get on with my work.

It doesn't even necessarily matter what my tasks are that day; I'm learning all the time, in a job I like, working with people I like, doing things that matter. And it gets me out of bed every morning.

That, or a dirty great bacon sandwich.

As I dropped my application for studying architecture into the mailbox I wasn't sure whether I would like to be an architect or not. I just did it because this was what I liked most at that time. I started my studies, made new friends, enjoyed my life, worked hard for my degree and never thought about studying something different. Every time I ask myself if it was, and still is the right way for me the answer is the same… I'm happy with what I'm doing. I spend a lot of time on projects; give as much as needed to grow ideas that there is no other decision for me. There is a lot to learn and there will be more to see and do in the future. The way I live as well as the way I feel is always a quest for me. This quest gets me out of bed every day. I don't know what the next day will bring, but to look forward to it with an open mind is how I try to live.

To be an architect can be more than just to draw lines. It's the way you act and the experiences you have which make the difference.

I get out of bed without thinking too much about it, usually about 6am. If anything I'm a morning person. There is always a measure of excitement and trepidation. Everyday there is something that has to be done; deadlines to meet, drawings to issue, legislation to comply with and people not to let down. This is what gets me out of bed.

Sometimes though, something very satisfying happens – like a good idea, resolving a detail, seeing a building grow from a sketch, or a very happy client – memorable because they don't happen everyday.

At these times I know why I still keep getting out of bed.

5.0

Sofia Pomares
Architectural
Assistant

Steve Wikeley
Graphic Designer

Tim Wenham
Architect

Vivien Boyle
Office Manager

What gets me out of bed? The question every human being asks to himself…

What gets me out of bed is probably what makes everyone else get out of bed: spending time with people, learning something new, remembering how much you laughed, having an idea, admiring someone, making a decision, sorting out a problem or just being comfortable.

…but what is particular about us is that once you are an architect, no matter what you see or do, you will always see it or do it as an architect.

I love to get up everyday to face the small challenges of the day. Daily I realise the more I learn the less I know, the more I want to know!

Although I love being in bed, with my duvet, my pillow – and my wife (although she's often up before I stir), I am driven from my slumber by: a sense of challenge, a sense of responsibility and a sense of expectation.

Working in architecture undoubtedly provides challenge, navigating the ever–shifting sands of opinion and regulations while not losing the idea. It offers a chance to make use of the skills and understanding that I have been gifted and taught and to fulfil my responsibility to those who have helped me and those I might help.

I can also always look forward to something unexpected from both my projects and my colleagues.

As I live close to the woods: the bloody birds that tweet and chirp through my window from 4am most mornings, as I have to get up to find the shotgun to scare them away!

But joking apart. Life gets me up, I want to see another day and learn something new, I want my son to come and tell me something that he has learnt and wants to share, I want to see the people I love, again and make them smile. I want to make a difference and you won't do that staying in bed!

It feels nice to get awards.
But all they feed is vanity.
So now that we have some,
we will seek them no more.

Acknowledgments

Text
Essays written by Irena Bauman.

Project pages written by
Irena Bauman, Simon Warren
and Guy Smith.

Articles written by
Matt Weaver, 'The truth about those iconic
buildings: the roofs leak, they're dingy and too
hot: Research finds Stirling prizewinners
'inadequate': 14 October 2006, © *Guardian
New and Media Ltd 2006.*

Richard Waite, 'Causeway for Concern', 21 July
2005, © *The Architects' Journal.*

Ellen Bennett, 'Competition re-run is next
chapter of library saga', 8 September 2006,
© *Building Design.*

Will Hurst, 'Simpson's contest boycott call
ignored', 26 August 2005, © *Building Design.*

Ellen Bennett, 'Rem demands boycott', 5
January 2007, © *Building Design.*

Zoe Blackler, 'The competitions gamble', 21
October 2005, © *Building Design.*

Patrick Lynch, 'Why is it so hard for young
architects?', 13 October 2006, © *Building
Design.*

Ellen Bennett, 'The great fat cat stitch up', 11
November 2005, © *Building Design.*

Charlie Gates, 'Profession takes a beating', 30
September 2005, © *Building Design.*

Photography
Irena Bauman (6, 41, 42, 48, 49, 53, 54, 55, 56,
57, 82, 129, 146, 185)
Bauman Lyons (74, 104, 112, 116, 180, 185, 186)
Arc Light (133)
Issa Bensalem (84, 85, 113, 151, 185)
Rachel Codling (4, 42, 44, 45, 47, 50, 51, 52,
55, 182, 182, 184, 185, 186, 187, 188, 189, 190)
Roderick Cyone (46)
Jonathan Davis (116)
Disney (Howard Roark 62)
Holbeck Regeneration Plan (154)
Nigel Gallagher (116)
Martine Hamilton-Knight (92, 104, 105,
109, 116, 117, 118, 119, 130, 131, 134, 135, 138,
139, 140, 141, 142, 143, 150, 178, 179, 181)
Vic Hinton (43, 93, 138, 139, 140, 141)
Leeds County Council (10, 44, 103, 169)
Eddie Marshal (52)
Casey Orr (124/125, 126, 127, 128)
Kate Parker (57)
Patrick Studios (130)
Martin Peters (84, 85, 147, 148)
RIBA Library Photographs Collection (88)
Collier Schorr (Cover, 2)
Guy Smith (118, 184)
Simon Warren (36, 37, 108, 188)
Marc Wilmot (144/155, 120/121)

Illustration
Rachel Codling (158, 160, 162, 164)
Iain Denby (154, 111, 115, 159, 161,
163, 165, 166, 175)
Andy Edwards (18, 25)
Matt Murphy (166)
Estell Warren (176, 177)